WAITING HEARTS
A story of extraordinary love

But they that wait upon the Lord
shall renew their strength.
They shall mount up with wings like eagles;
they shall run and not be weary;
they shall walk and not faint.
Isaiah 40:31

WAITING
HEARTS

Tom & Ginny Carr

a story of extraordinary love

Harold Shaw Publishers
Wheaton, Illinois

ISBN 0-87788-905-8

Library of Congress Cataloging-in-Publication Data
    Waiting hearts : a story of extraordinary love /Tom & Ginny Carr.
       p. cm.
    ISBN 0-87788-905-8
    1. Carr, Tom, 1946- . 2. Carr, Ginny. 3. Physically handicapped—United States—Biography. 4. Married people—United States—Biography. I. Carr, Ginny. II. Title.
HV3012.C36 1989
362.4′092′2—dc19
[B]   88-33706
                               CIP

---

98 97 96 95 94 93 92 91 90 89
10 9 8 7 6 5 4 3 2 1

To *the One*
who has written the Ultimate Love Story
in both our lives . . .
be all glory,
honor,
and praise.

Contents

Foreword

I am an incurable romantic, ready to light the candles for any dinner or wheel outside to enjoy a moonlit night. And for me, reading Tom and Ginny Carr's story is much like slowly browsing through a wedding album, or choosing a "just right" Valentine's card.

Waiting Hearts, however, is not like most romantic stories which flippantly say, "I love you . . . I'll do anything for you!" Rather, this is one story which says, "I love you . . . now let me prove it." And prove their love, they do—because God's power always shows up best through weakness.

Tom and Ginny have learned that love has little to do with one's physical appearance or abilities. They view their disabilities as the best asset in deepening love, stretching commitments, and enjoying life together. Love, for them, has more to do with words like sacrifice, honor, and duty.

Waiting Hearts is for anyone who questions how romance and love are linked together. It's for anyone whose emotions have worn thin as hardships in marriage have come and gone. It's for those who are still discovering that love is less of a feeling, and more of a commitment to action.

It's for you.

Joni Eareckson Tada

Tom and Ginny
Photo © 1986, Gus James

Preface

In the first month of our marriage, we shared our dreams—Tom's to write a book and Ginny's to develop her music ministry and make a flute record. Ginny had always said, "I'm a musician—not a writer." But on January 12, 1988, when Ramona Cramer Tucker informed us that Shaw Publishers wanted our story, we took it as a calling from the Lord; and for the next eight months, it became God's assignment to us.

Revealing our innermost thoughts and emotions has not been easy. But because we hoped our story might be an inspiration to others, we were willing to risk opening our hearts and to make ourselves vulnerable. We invite you to laugh and cry with us as we share not only our personal story, but also the legacy of Love that God has written in both our lives.

It is our prayer that this book would not only challenge you to peer more closely into your own heart, but that it would also encourage you to take a deeper look into the lives of those around you. 1 Samuel 16:7 (KJV) declares: ". . . for the Lord seeth not as man seeth; for man looketh on the outward appearance, but the Lord looketh on the heart." It's the labels we give people—short, tall, fat, skinny, race, nationality, mental or physical handicaps, etc.—that prevent us from seeing the real beauty in the hearts of others.

Though when we really stop to think about it, aren't most of us a bit handicapped in one way or another? Our handicaps can be visible or invisible, yet deep down inside, we all long to be accepted and loved with unconditional love.

In this age of superficial values and relationships, let's dare to be different. Let's dare to look past the externals and, with God's help, search for the rare and precious jewels we are sure to find in the hearts of others.

From our hearts to yours,
Tom and Ginny Carr

Acknowledgments

*... with our warmest thanks to each and every one
who helped us along on our journey toward publication.*

"You two should write a book." That comment, made by a lady from our church, after hearing us tell the story of our romance at a Valentine's Day luncheon, was the spark that started a book.

Not long after, I saw one of Norman Rohrer's advertisements in *Moody Monthly*. It said, "I Fire Writers." That ad primed the fire deep within my heart to write for the inspirational market. And Norman's recommendation that we attend the Forest Home Writers Conference in October 1983 added fuel to the fire.

At the conference we met Virginia Muir, senior editor of Tyndale House Publishers, and she encouraged us to keep writing—even though several other editors were pouring cold water on our plans to write a personal testimony book. But most importantly, she suggested we get some expert "hands on" help from Carole Gift Page, a prolific author and writing instructor living in Southern California. So under Carole's tutelage, and with the critiques of our writing class, a book proposal evolved.

In July 1986, at the Biola Writers Institute, Gloria Chisholm—an editor with *Aglow* magazine—encouraged us to press on when she bought the idea of an article I had written "if Ginny could rewrite it from her point of view." Ginny did . . . and the article (along with our picture on the cover) appeared in the May/June 1987 issue of *Aglow*.

Then at the 1987 Biola Writers Institute, two more writing experts, Lee Roddy and Stan Baldwin, reviewed our revised book proposal. Their critiques helped us to fine tune and sharpen the focus of our story.

That same summer Joe Davis, Executive Director of Joni & Friends, introduced us to Steve Board and Randy Jahns of Harold Shaw Publishers. We corresponded with Randy and with Ramona Cramer Tucker—HSP editorial director—and in January 1988 a contract was signed. Since then, Ramona has been invaluable in helping and guiding us to the completion of this project.

And of course, we owe special thanks to our families and all the people mentioned in the book—as well as to many who may not have made it through the final edit—for the roles they have played in our lives. Thanks also to Rev. Eugene and Jean Coffin, whose marriage has been a shining example of two people working as one in serving the Lord.

But most importantly, thanks go to Ginny, the wonderful woman who lovingly labored by my side—in spite of all the stresses of overseeing a household with two physically challenged people—to complete this book. Reliving and writing out our love story, though it has not been easy, has been one of the most fulfilling and rewarding things we have ever done together.

Tom Carr

1
Knight in Shining Armor

Ginny

The Sunday evening service had just begun when a late-arriving man in a wheelchair rolled by and parked in the aisle two pews ahead of me. As he faced the pulpit, I noticed his handsome profile. His mustache matched the color of his hair—dark brown flecked with gray. In navy-blue slacks, vest, and matching tie, he looked very distinguished, and his features were tanned with California sun. *A successful businessman*, I guessed.

Who was he? He'd rolled in alone, and I couldn't help wondering, *Where is his girlfriend—or wife?* Maybe he was single, but even if he was, how could I ever hope to meet him? Oh well, at least I could dream.

Only a few moments before, the music minister had exhorted, "Let's begin with the joyous hymn 'Make Me a Blessing.'" I had mumbled the first few lines, but then I couldn't sing anymore. My heart just wasn't in it. All my life people had told me what a blessing I was. I'd prayed that

God would use me in the lives of others—being a blessing had been my goal. I'd served as a deaconess and also on the Missions Board at church. My service to the Lord was usually a source of great joy for me, but tonight I was discouraged. Being a blessing couldn't change the facts: I was lonely.

I'd played my flute in the weddings of many friends and wondered if my "knight in shining armor" would ever come along. One by one, each of my five roommates had fallen in love and gotten married—but romance eluded me. At thirty-four, I'd never even had a steady boyfriend. This evening I could no longer sing that song or pray that prayer. With tears streaming down my cheeks, I pleaded, *Lord, I don't want to be a blessing anymore. All I want to be is a plain old ordinary girl who some plain old ordinary guy can love.* Then, through the blur of my tears, I had seen the man in the wheelchair move past me on the left.

I couldn't help it—soon my focus was shifting back and forth between the stranger and what was happening on the platform. I tried to concentrate as the short-term missionaries were commissioned for their summer service, reflecting on my own experiences as a short-termer. A year after receiving my bachelor's degree in medical technology, I had flown halfway around the world to set up a medical laboratory at the new Evangelical Free Church Hospital in Hong Kong. It was my first airplane flight ever—how excited I'd been! My year and a half there was full of challenge. Now I missed that adventurous feeling. *Why can't I be single and happy anymore?* I wondered, and I looked again at that handsome profile.

As the service progressed, I found myself paying more attention to the man in the wheelchair than to the program. A red and blue bag hanging on the back of his wheelchair

Ginny
1981

caught my eyes. It was beautifully embroidered with a white dove and the words "PRAISE THE LORD—GOD LOVES US." *His girlfriend probably made that for him,* I guessed. *Stop dreaming, Ginny!*

But the more I watched him, the more curious I became. He removed a pad of paper from the bag and began to write continuously. *He must be a committed Bible student to be taking so many notes,* I thought. Then, during the closing prayer, I prayed rather desperately, *Oh Lord, at least let him say hello!* This new face had distracted me from my own struggle, and I had a new, hopeful feeling. But meeting him really wasn't very likely. More than a thousand people were leaving the sanctuary all at once. He probably wouldn't even notice me.

As the church cleared, he made no effort to move. He just sat there looking around as if he were searching for someone. Finally, he turned up the aisle and I saw him face-to-face. *He looks like Omar Sharif!* I thought, checking out his dark mustache. I sat stiffly in the pew, my heart pounding, as he rolled up the aisle in my direction. I was paralyzed as I saw my hour of dreamy infatuation about to vanish. In a matter of minutes I'd gone from the depths of despair to the heights of hope, and now only God could work his plan.

"Hi! How are you tonight?" he asked, as his eyes met mine. He was talking to me! Could he tell that I'd been crying? For once I was glad that the ring finger of my left hand was bare. I panicked. *What should I do now?* I groped for a response, but no words came.

"Sorry—did I interrupt your thoughts?" he asked, as he pulled his wheelchair next to my pew. Before I could pull myself together and reply, I saw his eyes look across the emptying sanctuary again, searching for someone. Who?

But his attention soon came back to me. "My name's Tom. What's yours?"

"Oh! I'm Ginny." I blurted out the words.

"The Fullerton Free Church sure is a big place. How do you ever find anyone here?"

"Are you looking for someone special?" I asked. "Maybe I can help you." He looked straight at me, and I thought about how awful I must look, my makeup tear-stained and smudged. "You're so tan," I rushed on, grasping for conversation. "Did you go to the beach today?"

"Not exactly the beach. I spent the day sailing with my best friend and his family."

"It must be great to have a friend to go sailing with."

"It is. I work with Hugo, but he's really more like a brother. His wife Ellen even made this wheelchair bag for me," he said, as he took it off the chair and showed it to me.

"It's beautiful. I was admiring it during the service." If he only knew I'd been admiring *him* more than the bag, I wonder what he would have thought. "By the way, where do you work?"

"I'm a nuclear/environmental engineer with Bechtel Power Corporation," he smiled back at me. "But I mainly give speeches about the energy crisis these days—and what new energy sources we have available to meet our needs."

"I don't think I've ever heard of Bechtel."

"We try to keep a low profile, but we're actually the biggest engineering firm in the world," he announced. He looked so proud—as if he'd made a major declaration.

Wow, I thought, *an engineer. So he's a technical person too. Maybe we'll have something to talk about.*

Tom glanced beneath the pew. "I hope you don't mind my asking, but I see that you have crutches and a leg brace. Do you have Multiple Sclerosis?"

"No . . . I had polio when I was a little girl." I didn't mind his asking—I was thrilled just to be talking with him.

"You must have had a pretty bad case," Tom went on as he applied the brakes to keep his wheelchair from rolling backwards down the aisle.

"I was paralyzed from my neck down at first, and I'm thankful to be alive. But what about you? Were you in an accident?"

"No," he paused, "I've had MS since 1970. I walked with crutches for a year, too. But since 1973 I've been using a wheelchair full-time. It sure makes life a lot easier."

"Full-time? Then how do you stay in such great shape?" I couldn't help but notice his muscular upper body.

"Actually, I used to be very athletic—tennis was my forte. But now I keep my upper body in shape because it's my arms that get me to places where my legs used to take me," he replied. He was friendly enough, but his eyes kept looking toward the back of the sanctuary. Who was he searching for?

"By the way, do you attend here regularly? I've never seen you before," I said, trying to get his attention.

"This is my first time. I came looking for a friend, but I had no idea how hard it would be to find her. The congestion here is worse than at the Los Angeles Coliseum!"

"Oh. What's your girlfriend's name?" I realized that my dream of an eligible young man had just been punctured.

"Oh, she's not my girlfriend. Pam gave me one of Chuck Swindoll's tapes and invited me to visit the church sometime. I'm disappointed Swindoll wasn't here tonight."

"He usually is, but I think he's away speaking at a conference this weekend." Inside I was happy and excited again. At least she wasn't his girl.

"Are you a member of the career group here?" Tom continued.

"Well, I was active in the class for about eight years, but being a deaconess takes up most of my time now."

Tom seemed impressed, and his tone brightened. "Ginny, I have to go. But I hope to see you again. Here's my business card. I often speak to singles groups. Call me if you'd ever like me to come and speak to yours."

"About what?" I asked him. My heart pounded, and my face felt flushed. He was preparing to leave. Was I winning or losing my dream?

"About the Lord, of course. He's the ultimate energy source." Tom winked. "I'll even give you my home phone number."

Wondering what he meant by that, I went on, "Thanks. Maybe I'll see you here again sometime." Then I stretched out my right leg and locked my brace with a sharp snap. It was time to go and already the few minutes I'd known Tom had been like a rollercoaster ride. He had been kind to stop and talk, but now he was throwing the ball back to me for the next move. Was he simply looking for an "in" at the church? Befriending him might turn out to be an expensive emotional gamble—too expensive.

"I'd offer to take you out for coffee or ice cream," he said as I stood up, "but I'm trying to stay away from caffeine and sugar."

"Why? You certainly don't look like you have a weight problem."

"No, that's not it. Caffeine and sugar are bad for people with MS. If you can think of something else we might get for a snack, I'll go for it."

"How about a salad? That would be pretty healthy, wouldn't it?" I said, beginning my slow walk up the aisle. He rolled his chair next to me, matching my pace. I tried not to get my hopes up, but I'd always dreamed that someday I'd find a man who walked at my speed.

"And I know the perfect place! They've got a twenty-foot long salad bar."

He was actually asking me out. I could hardly believe it.

"Let's get my car, and I'll show you the most fantastic view in Fullerton on our way there," Tom added.

"Great! But let me go and freshen up first," I replied, turning toward the ladies' lounge. "I'll just be a minute."

Romantic thoughts danced in my head as I looked in the mirror. I felt so happy and light-hearted now that I could hardly believe I'd been so discouraged. Just two hours ago, in this same lounge, I had wondered why I had come to church. I had even debated whether or not to trudge back to my car and go home. But something had compelled me to stay.

How ironic that at a time when I thought I looked and felt my worst, God would bring along such a wonderful surprise. I wondered what the days ahead might hold. *But for now,* I thought, *I'll just enjoy every minute of this evening.*

My spirits soared as I stepped out into the warm spring air and saw Tom sitting in his top-down Mustang convertible. He certainly wasn't the plain old ordinary fellow I'd asked God for during the service. And when I'd thought of shining armor, I'd never imagined a wheelchair. This was already a never-to-be-forgotten evening, and it had only just begun!

2

Make Me a Blessing

Tom

Strange, isn't it? I thought, as I sat in the car and watched Ginny walk from the church lobby toward me. I'd never have guessed, only a few hours ago, that instead of meeting Pam, the girl of my dreams, I'd find this sad-faced little crippled girl.

The evening had two strikes against it—no Swindoll, no Pam. I had been looking forward to hearing the well-known pastor speak, yet he wasn't there; so I'd spent the sermon time preparing a presentation I had to give the next week.

But I'd been hoping even more to see Pam. She was special to me. We'd met about five years before at Garden Grove Community Church (GGCC) and were "Hi, how are you?" Sunday morning friends. The one time I'd worked up the nerve to ask her out, she'd mentioned that she took "daily walks with Jesus." I hadn't pursued her any further since I wasn't even taking "weekly rolls with Jesus" back then.

We'd lost contact for about three years and during that time a lot of things changed: GGCC had become the Crystal Cathedral, Pam was attending the Fullerton Evangelical

Free Church, and I had invited God to become a personal part of my life. Then I bumped into her again, and we began to do a few things together. She came to hear me speak at church and helped me host a brunch at my condo. Last month I'd even taken her to a concert. Although it was a lukewarm first date, the future seemed bright. I was sure God had renewed our friendship for a reason.

I had hoped I might see her at the Free Church tonight. But it wasn't really very likely in that crowd. And even if I had found her, she probably would have been going out with other friends after the service. Hoping to see Pam had been a longshot at best.

But Ginny had breathed new life into the evening. This petite young woman in her pink peasant dress looked like a department-store doll—except for the leg brace and crutches. Ginny seemed to have those "three-day weekend blues"—single and nobody to share the holiday with—when I'd met her a half hour before. But now she'd done a complete turnaround. She was walking toward the car, every step an effort, yet her face was beaming. She looked like a girl who'd just received her first bouquet of roses. *Tomorrow is Memorial Day, and I don't have to work, I thought. I'll just relax and try to be a blessing to her.*

"You got here so quickly!" she said as she approached my car. "I'm sorry to keep you waiting."

"That's okay. I'm sure you're worth waiting for," I smiled, leaning across the seat to open the door for her.

"A convertible! And I love your license plate. U-R-O-K-2—that's great!"

"I got it with hopes that it would be an encouragement to people. Ever ridden in a convertible?"

"In high school," she nodded, as she stepped into the car and pulled the door shut. "That was a special time, too."

Tom
1980

"Really?" I said, questioning to keep the conversation going.

She smiled back at me. "I rode in one when I was my high school Homecoming Queen. It sure was fun."

"*Homecoming Queen!* Wow! I don't think I can match that for excitement."

"Well, it really was a special time in my life, but so is tonight. It's not everyday I get to go out with someone as handsome as you."

Her compliment made me feel good. "And it's not every day that I get to go out with a homecoming queen either," I replied. I'd dated some beautiful girls, but Ginny was the first official queen.

"Where did you go to high school?" I asked.

"In Winona, a city of about 25,000 in southern Minnesota. It's an incredibly beautiful place—right in the Mississippi River Valley."

"It sounds like you work for the Winona Chamber of Commerce," I teased her. "How did a Minnesota girl ever wind up in Southern California?"

"I went to Hong Kong as a short-term missionary in the late sixties. After spending two winters there with no snow to trudge through, I realized that living in a more moderate climate would be easier for me. So when I returned to the States, I moved to California. How about you?" she asked, as I cruised slowly up the hill.

"I'm from North Tonawanda, New York—near Niagara Falls. I came out here to go to college."

The evening air ruffled her hair as we stopped at the top for a red light, catching a panoramic view of Orange County. The lights of Anaheim to the right sparkled like a fairyland,

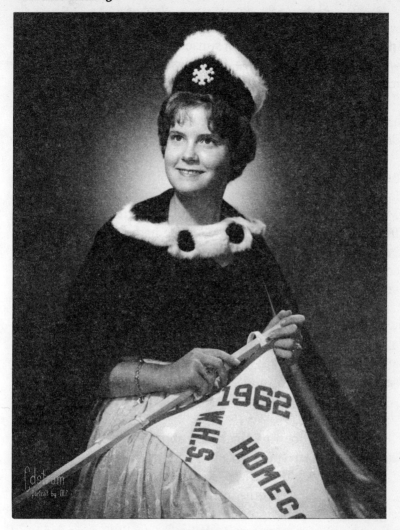

Ginny Holty
Winona High School Homecoming Queen
©1962 Edstrom Portrait by Alf

while behind us the skyscrapers of Los Angeles were bathed in a brilliant reddish-golden sunset. I'd always thought this would be a romantic drive, and it was nice to see the confirmation in Ginny's face.

"Do you see that tall, glowing cross in the distance?" I asked. "That's the Crystal Cathedral. I usually go there Sunday evenings."

A few minutes later, we pulled into a dimly lit parking lot next to a quaint old brick building. Elmer's Place, an old-fashioned country restaurant, was a real favorite of mine. Maybe it was the casual Alpine ambiance that warmed me from the inside out every time I came here. It had an open-beamed, lofty ceiling, and an open kitchen decorated with copper and brick. The oak tables were decked with checkered cloth napkins and candles.

We moved into the entryway where a cheery young waitress escorted us into the dining area, right across the aisle from the salad bar. I watched Ginny as she looked around. She seemed to be absorbing the sights, sounds, and smells of every nook and cranny in the place.

"Let's start with blueberry soup," I suggested.

"What's that?"

"Pureed blueberries, thickened and served in a cup. You eat it with a soup spoon. Want to try it?"

"Sure. I love blueberries."

The waitress took our order, and Ginny continued, "My eighty-four-year-old grandmother lives in Maine in an area where wild blueberries grow. When I was little she used to go berry picking in the woods and make fresh pie for us. But she never made soup out of them!"

By the time we'd finished our "blueberry soup," Ginny was a believer. "This is great! I've got to tell Grandma Agda about it the next time I talk to her." I watched her in wonder. The sad-faced crippled girl I had met in church had turned into an enthusiastic, pretty young woman.

"And you ain't seen nothing yet!" I exclaimed. Then I rolled across the aisle to the twenty-foot-long salad bar and proceeded to build a huge salad for us to share.

"This is going to be the greatest, most perfectly symmetrical salad you've ever seen," I announced as I dipped into bowls of cauliflower, broccoli, and carrots, carefully placing two of each on opposite sides of the plate.

"It's a work of art," she said when I rolled back, balancing the plate on my lap. "You really *are* an engineer. How can I ever dig into such a masterpiece?"

"You'd better! If you don't eat your half, I will. Let's pray," I said, reaching over to take her hand. "Dear Lord, we thank you for this beautiful day and all our abundant blessings. Help us each to remember that we are blessed to be a blessing. Amen. Dig in!"

"Where do you work?" I asked Ginny as we ate. I wasn't sure if she did, since walking seemed to be quite difficult for her.

"I'm a medical technologist in charge of the Microbiology Department at Coast Clinical Lab in Anaheim. I'm the one who puts the bugs to bed at night!"

I chuckled. "Wow! Sounds like an important job. But don't you get exhausted being on the go and working all day? It looks like getting around is pretty tough for you."

"Yes, I do get tired. I don't have the energy to do much after work on workdays."

"I know what you mean. I get tired, too. But would you believe my boss lets me take twenty-minute naps every afternoon? One time when I was in the hospital, the nuclear group even sent me a card that said, 'Hurry up and get well. We miss your snoring at the office.' "

"That's neat," Ginny said, laughing. "They must really love you."

"Bechtel's great—especially because the people are wonderful. But what about you? What do you like to do in your spare time?"

"Right now, I'm taking care of five little kittens."

"Your cat gave you a new family, eh?"

"No. Someone just left them in the brick planter outside my apartment window last week," she said with a shy grin. "They can't be much more than a week old."

"Now, why in the world would anybody do that?"

"Someone knows I have a soft heart."

I smiled. Her compassion for the little creatures touched me.

"Tom, would you pray that I'll be able to find good homes for them?" she asked hesitantly.

I nodded. "Sure I will." Now this was something new! No girl had ever asked me to pray about cats before. *This Ginny is something else,* I said to myself.

Finishing the last red cherry tomato, I asked Ginny cautiously, "How do you get around when you travel? Walking looks pretty tough for you."

"You sure seem worried about that," she responded, with a hint of irritation in her voice. "I've used crutches for thirty years. I'm thankful I can walk. And when I get tired, I just sit down."

I ignored the defensive edge in her words. "I know what you mean. I limped around with crutches for a year before I learned how much a wheelchair could help. I have a spare one," I said, trying to sound matter-of-fact. "Why don't you borrow it? It would really make things a lot easier for you."

"No, thanks, I'll be fine," she responded firmly.

"I used to feel the same way. I thought the wheelchair was my enemy at first. But the Lord showed me that it really was my friend."

"How interesting," Ginny said politely. Then she changed the subject. "How did you find the Lord, Tom?"

"Slowly, but surely. I wanted to be a Lutheran minister when I was young. I even took three years of Latin in high school!"

"You did? So did I!"

"But I got distracted. I became a 'Sputnik' kid."

"'Sputnik' kid?"

"The Russians launched their first space craft—they called it 'Sputnik'—when I was in grade school. I was put in advanced math and science classes and encouraged to become a technical person."

"Wow. You must be some kind of genius."

"Not really. But I did get a perfect 800 score on the College Boards in Advanced Math. A lot of scholarship offers came from that."

"So what did you do?"

"What any young tennis player from a poor family in frigid North Tonawanda, New York would do—forget about the ministry, come out to Harvey Mudd College in California, and play tennis all year around."

"I'm glad you moved to California," Ginny said, flashing me her pixie smile as I looked into her hazel eyes. She seemed like a sister or a good friend—she was so easy to talk with. I liked that, but I wondered if she was reading too much into our time together.

"I am too. But moving to California made it easy for me to leave God and my Bible back in North Tonawanda. It was only when MS forced me to abandon my fun-in-the-sun lifestyle that I came back to the Lord."

"But you did, right?"

"All the way back and then some. I started attending Robert Schuller's drive-in church in '74 . . ."

"A drive-in church!" Ginny interrupted. "What's that?"

"Schuller's open air church. I'd just drive into the parking lot wearing my T-shirt and bermuda shorts, put my convertible top down and be fed spiritually without leaving my car."

"Well, thank goodness for Dr. Schuller," Ginny chuckled. "Since it's hard for my grandma to get out to church anymore, she watches him on television every Sunday."

"My whole attitude about MS turned around when I heard Pastor Schuller say 'there's opportunity in adversity.' I started to get involved in the singles fellowship and took a two-year Bethel Bible Teachers training class.

"Then in 1977 I even won a fellowship and attended seminary part-time for two quarters . . ."

"You two seem to be having a great time, but we're closing now," the manager interrupted.

I couldn't believe how quickly the time had flown by. We looked around and laughed. All the tables were empty and laid out with clean settings for Monday's lunch crowd.

The moon was bright and the scent of orange blossoms lingered in the air as we drove back to the church. Ginny seemed to radiate as she thanked me over and over for the salad we'd shared. She was one of the nicest girls I'd ever met. And our evening had been special, without the trite, jockeying type of conversation that most first meetings entailed. Instead, she had been honestly interested in me.

As Ginny prepared to go to her car, she looked at me thoughtfully and asked, "Would it be all right if I give you a hug? This has been such a wonderful evening."

I was surprised! Here was a girl who had changed from sad and lonely to sweet and lovely in one short evening. Though my heart was touched by her apparent need for friendship, an uneasiness enveloped me. It was obviously a night to remember for her, but I couldn't let her think it was anything more than a "split salad" night for me.

I purposely did not ask for her phone number . . . I didn't want her to expect some future contact. But a hug could be even more misleading. After all, even casual hugs weren't something girls naturally gave me. Whether it was the inconvenience of climbing across the metal wheelchair or getting their dresses dirty on the tires, most girls chose to shake my hand.

Now the tables were turned, and I was withholding a casual hug from Ginny. Was it because she was far too nice—and far too fragile—for me? Was it because a cold good-bye now would bring her less pain in the long run? Or was it that it had been a wonderful evening, and I feared becoming friends with a handicapped woman?

She waited, her eyes longing for something—maybe just a vote of confidence or an affirmation of her value as a woman.

Reaching over to her seat, I put my hand on hers. It had been almost four years since I'd felt the acceptance Ginny was offering me. I didn't know what tomorrow would hold, but perhaps for tonight that hug might be good for both of us.

3

Lord, Watch Over My Heart

Ginny

The morning sun streamed through my windows, but I lingered in bed, watching the gleaming rays dance across the carpet toward me. This Monday I was basking not only in the bright sunshine, but also in the warm glow of last night. I could still feel Tom's strong arms encircling me as we sat there in his car. He seemed to enjoy the moment as much as I did.

Had I been too forward in asking if I could give him a hug, I wondered? Would it scare him away from any further friendship with me? And what had made him suddenly draw away and then become so distant? It almost seemed as if he had caught himself enjoying our embrace too much.

But the best part of the whole evening was when Tom suggested that we pray together. I had just asked if I could give him a hug. And after a few moments of silence, he had responded, "Ginny, it's been such a beautiful evening. Why don't we pray together before we say good night?" I figured he was stalling for time—trying to decide what to do.

Then he reached over and took my hand in his. And the warmth I felt between us as we lifted our hearts to God made me feel so close to this man. All my life I'd longed for a man with whom I could pray and really share my heart.

I lay in bed wondering if I would ever see Tom again. He had offered to lend me his spare wheelchair. It seemed strange that he would offer his chair and then say nothing about seeing me again.

I thought again about using the chair. Certainly there were times when it would come in handy. But how would I get it up and down the five steps leading to my apartment building? And it was surely too heavy to lift in and out of my car trunk by myself.

No, I wouldn't accept the wheelchair. I couldn't bear it if that were the only time I'd see Tom—when he came to visit his chair! And I didn't want to be storing any borrowed equipment I'd have to return if our friendship didn't last.

All day long I kept hoping that Tom would call—even though I knew he didn't have my phone number. Disappointed that he hadn't asked me for it, I prayed that somehow he'd remember my last name and look it up. I wanted so much to talk with him—just to hear his voice. How surprising it was to feel so much for a man with whom I'd only spent one evening! I tried to keep myself from hoping too much.

By 6:00 o'clock, I could stand it no longer. I got out the business card he'd given me and dialed the number written on the back. *Why am I doing this?* I thought. *What will Tom think of me? I must be crazy.*

The phone rang six or seven times, but I knew that it might take Tom longer to get to the phone because he was in a wheelchair.

"Hello, Tom Carr here," his voice echoed through the phone.

"Hi, Tom. This is Ginny." I felt nervous but thrilled to find him at home.

"Ginny?"

"Virginia Holty," I reminded him. *Great*, I thought, *he's already forgotten me!* "We met at church last night. Remember?"

"Oh, sure. How are you?"

"I'm doing great!" I answered in one breath. "I just wanted to thank you once again for a fun evening."

"You didn't have to do that. It was no big deal. Besides, you thanked me a half dozen times during the drive back to the church."

"Did I?" I laughed. "Well, I sure enjoyed it a lot."

"I thought you'd be out celebrating the holiday with friends tonight."

"And I thought you'd be doing the same."

We chatted for almost a half hour, and when I hung up, I felt wonderful. We talked and shared so easily. But would I ever hear from him again? He still hadn't asked for my phone number.

A week passed, and I went to church the following Sunday evening, hoping to see him there—even though I knew it was a long shot. He didn't show up, and I was disappointed. All the excitement of the previous week had disappeared—like the air in a deflated balloon.

Returning to my empty apartment after church, I decided to put my heart out on the line again. I tried calling Tom, but

all I got was his answering machine: "Hello, this is Tom
Carr. Thank you for calling. I'm sorry, but I'm not able to get
to the telephone right now. If you'll leave your name and
number and as long a message as you like, with the date and
time of your call, I'll call you back as soon as I get the
message. God loves you, and so do I."

I hung up without leaving a message and called again just
to listen to his voice: "God loves you, and so do I."

Forget him, I told myself, as a familiar feeling of hopeless-
ness flooded over me. I shouldn't be calling him like this.
Why couldn't I get Tom Carr off my mind? What was wrong
with me anyway?

The ache in my heart made it clear to me—I'd already
fallen in love with Tom. *Lord, show me what to do*, I prayed
silently. *I need your guidance. Are these feelings just my own, or
did you put them in my heart?*

Suddenly, an idea came to mind. I remembered Tom
saying how much he appreciated home-cooked meals.
Maybe I could invite him over for dinner. My spirits soared
as I thought about the fun I would have fixing him a special
meal. But it would take a lot of courage for me to ask him.

Then doubts began to creep in. Should I risk loving him?
Should I risk even being friends? I knew I had to count the
cost. If our friendship didn't work out, would I be able to
bear the pain of rejection I knew I'd experience? Was it
worth the gamble?

Show me, Lord, I prayed again. *Somehow, show me what to
do*.

At my bedside lay the book I'd been reading, *Perfect Peace*
by Charles L. Allen. I flipped to where I'd placed my book-
mark several weeks ago and stared in amazement at the
bold-face print halfway down the page. The words seemed
to jump off the paper at me: "Love Takes a Chance." I read

on: "If you are not willing to take a chance on loving some-body, then you will never be hurt, no matter what might happen. If you love a person, then you take the chance of being hurt."

I knew God had answered my prayer. Whether our relationship became anything lasting or not, I was sure loving Tom would be worth the risk.

4

Hollywood, Here I Come!

Ginny

On Monday afternoon I called Tom at work to invite him over for dinner the following week. We settled on a date, but he said he'd call back to confirm it after checking his schedule further. Finally he asked for my phone number.

He called two days later.

"Ginny, this is Tom. How are you today?"

"I'm great. I just went shopping for all the groceries for our dinner."

"Oh, Ginny, you're something else! I wish you hadn't done that."

"But why not? I wanted to get a head start on making you a scrumptious, sugar-free barbecue rib dinner. Isn't that your favorite?"

"Yes, it's my favorite, but I'm going to have to break our date. I've been asked to make a T.V. show that night. Can you find someone else to have over?"

"Oh, Tom. I was really looking forward to making dinner for *you*," I blurted out, unable to hide the disappointment in my voice.

"I know, but business is business. This is the kind of thing Bechtel pays me to do."

"What channel and what time? At least then I can see my almost-dinner-guest-T.V.-star in action."

"It's not being shown live; it's being taped. It'll probably come out in a couple of months. I'll call you when I know the details."

My heart sank again. It was over already. I just knew it. He would never call back. I braced myself for the worst and prepared to let it go at that.

Then I could hardly believe my ears. "How would you like to go to the T.V. studio with me, Ginny? It's a program about handicapped people. You might like it."

"Oh, Tom! Do you mean it? I'd love to."

"Mondays are your days off, right?"

"Right. What's the name of the program?"

"They call it "It Can Be Done." I think Joni Eareckson was on it a while back too."

"Oh—do you know Joni?"

"I've met her. We both received Mainstream Milestones awards last January. The awards were given by the Los Angeles Junior Chamber of Commerce to outstanding hand-icapped achievers."

"Congratulations, Tom! That is quite an honor."

"It *was*. I'll tell you about it when I pick you up next Monday afternoon. See you then."

"I'll be ready. Have a great week."

The next few days were exciting. I told my friends at work about the "special new guy" who'd invited me to go with him to make a T.V. show. I told them he was tall, dark, and handsome—and that he looked like Omar Sharif. But I didn't mention that he was confined to a wheelchair.

The big day arrived, and I was up early. Thoughts of the evening ahead danced through my mind. But doubts crept in. Looking at my limp right leg, I wondered if Tom would mind being seen at the T.V. studio with a handicapped young woman as his date. Then grabbing my crutches with new resolve, I determined to look as beautiful as I ever had. "Watch out, Hollywood. Here I come!" I declared aloud.

Fingering my way through the closet, I realized I'd never even worn some of the dresses hanging there. Like a chipmunk storing nuts for the winter months, I'd been saving them for special occasions. *I should have asked Tom what to wear,* I thought. What would be appropriate and still catch his attention?

"This is it!" I exclaimed out loud, as I pulled my pastel floral and black dress out of the closet. My parents had bought it for me two years ago. "This will be perfect." After all, Tom had said that we might go out for a nice dinner afterwards. And the dress I'd chosen was tea length and would cover up most of my brace—I wanted to look as normal as possible. But when I looked at my two wooden crutches I knew that there was no way to cover them up.

How I wished I could wear a pair of high heels like other girls—instead of my low thick-heeled shoes, the only kind that would accommodate my leg brace. These were things about me that I couldn't change. Hopefully, Tom would accept me the way I really was.

It was unusual for me to feel so self-conscious about my physical appearance. I had always believed that people didn't want to be impressed—they just wanted to be loved.

And I had tried to live my life that way. But I'd never wanted to impress anyone as much as I wanted to impress Tom. I would do everything I could to make him feel proud and glad he'd invited me.

5

The Big Performance

Ginny

Butterflies swirled in my stomach. I had never been so nervous in my entire life—not even in the ninth grade when I'd played my very first flute solo, "Flight of the Bumble Bee," in front of a thousand people. *Tonight will be my biggest performance ever,* I thought, *and it will be only for one. Oh Lord, please help me to win Tom's heart.*

At two P.M. sharp a horn sounded outside. I couldn't keep from chuckling. *Isn't this the way it used to be in high school?* Tom had told me it would be too much of a hassle for him to get out of the car just to knock on the door, so he'd honk when he arrived.

Tom smiled and waved as I started up the five steps leading to the sidewalk. He watched intently as I held the railing tightly, lifting first my left leg and then swinging my right leg up each step. His gaze made me feel uncomfortable, and I wondered what he was thinking. I wasn't used to being under such scrutiny. But I just smiled back at him, hoping my smile would outshine my awkward gait.

"Ginny, you look beautiful," he said, reaching over to push open the car door for me. "And you're so courageous. Just watching you climb those steps brings tears to my eyes."

"It does? Why?"

"It brings back memories of some pretty tough times when I struggled with crutches, too," he said, his sensitive brown eyes looking directly into mine.

He looked so handsome in his Westchester plaid, three-piece suit, and there was even a faint scent of musk in the air. *Is that for the television audience—or for me?* I wondered.

"But Ginny, how did you think I was ever going to get into your place with all those steps? I can't walk with crutches anymore."

"Oh Tom! I never even thought about those steps. But when you come for dinner, I can help you down the hill. Or I can ask my neighbors to take you down the steps. I wasn't even thinking about your wheelchair."

"I don't know if it will work, Ginny," he said, with a perplexed look. "But let's go. We don't want to be late to the studio."

As I thought about it—it was pretty naive of me to think I could push him up or down the grassy incline next to my apartment building.

"That award you and Joni won . . . you must have done something really special," I commented, as we sped onto the freeway and headed toward Hollywood.

"It wasn't just us. There were ten awards in all. The best part was being able to share with the audience—three hundred business leaders and their spouses—about the strength Christ gives me to overcome my limitations."

"How did you manage that?"

"When the emcee gave me the plaque and shook my hand, I asked him if I could say a word. He told me to go ahead but keep it short. Do you want me to tell you what I said? I can repeat it verbatim."

"Fire away, Tom. I'm listening." I could sense he really wanted to tell me.

Tom smiled and cleared his throat, as if he were actually there giving his speech all over again. "After thanking them for my award, I said: 'I hope that what I say here tonight will comfort those of you who are afflicted—but I also hope it will afflict those of you who are comfortable.' Then I quoted Helen Keller who said, 'I am thankful for my handicaps. Through them I have come to know myself, my work, and my God.' And I finished by saying, 'I feel much the same way. Because of Multiple Sclerosis I have come to know Tom Carr better, to know and love my employer, Bechtel Power Corporation, and to know and accept Jesus Christ as my Lord and personal Savior. I hope that each of you are as blessed as I am.' "

"That's a beautiful testimony, Tom."

"You should have heard Joni's. When she received her award, she told how what she had to bear was really very minor, compared to what Jesus suffered on the cross for her. Since then, Joni and I have become friends," he said proudly.

"Have you seen her lately?"

"Last Friday."

"You did?" I asked, trying not to sound too curious. "What for?" My first thought was that Tom was interested in Joni, and I was out. *Next to Joni*, I thought, *I don't stand a chance.*

"I proposed to her," he teased, "but not in the marriage sense—though that wouldn't be a bad idea. She's a beautiful woman. We talked about my idea for a Handicap Awareness Sunday, when churches all over the country would recognize the contributions and needs of the handicapped in their churches and communities."

"What a good idea," I said, breathing a sigh of relief.

When we arrived at the station, Tom parked next to the building and we went right in. The studio was small, with only two stages and a few offices—all on one floor.

Tom was immediately escorted to the make-up room, and I waited off stage. I'd never been in a T.V. studio before and everything about it interested me. There were four huge cameras on the set and cables all over the floor. High-powered lamps hung above a simple setting with a couch, two chairs and a number of green plants. On T.V. it would look neat and organized; yet behind the scenes, it seemed that disarray reigned.

"O.K., Ginny, do I look like a T.V. star?" Tom asked, as he returned from the make-up room.

To me, he looked like he belonged on a Hollywood movie set—not in a wheelchair.

"You look great. Are you nervous?"

"Not really. I've done a lot of T.V. interviews for Bechtel in the past four years. But let's pray quickly and commit this interview to God," he suggested. He took my hand and bowed his head.

Before we finished praying, one of the stage crew came over to direct Tom to his position on the set. He pointed me toward the lounge where I'd be able to watch the taping on a television monitor.

"Beethoven was handicapped . . . and yet he composed some of the greatest music the world has ever known," the sound track boomed out. At the same time, a portrait of Beethoven filled the screen while one of his symphonies played in the background. The sound track continued . . . "It Can Be Done."

Then an attractive woman and a distinguished gentleman, both sitting in plush chairs at the center of the stage, appeared on the monitor. Tom had explained to me that Mildred Kritt, who co-hosted with Ted Meyers, was the founder of this weekly program. I observed that Mildred also had a handicap—a prosthetic arm.

"This is a show about handicaps and people who have overcome their handicaps," Ted announced. "Today's guest is Thomas L. Carr, P.E.—professional engineer," he read from Tom's resume. "Engineering degree from Harvey Mudd College . . . Masters degree in Operations Research from USC." Then Tom's smiling face appeared on the monitor. He looked like a young executive, and his wheelchair was not visible in the waist-up camera shot. "This says you're a nuclear engineer and that you've also attended seminary," Ted noted, "and you're also the Division Public Affairs coordinator for the Bechtel Power Corporation. Is being here today part of your job, Tom?"

Tom raised his eyebrows and looked directly into the camera. "No, I wouldn't say it's specifically part of my job. In my job I go out and share with the public about the energy situation here in the United States and in the world— and about how we can try to resolve some of our energy shortage problems with new energy alternatives."

"Tom, you sound like a pretty busy man. You have quite a hard job ahead of you, I'd say. I'm sure there must be a certain amount of resistance to your "preachments"—I mean the technical ones, not your theological ones. Do you find much resistance to those or not?"

Tom chuckled. "Well, I think the Lord uniquely trained me for my theological "preachments" by putting me in the nuclear energy field. Certainly the opposition we've received there has helped me to become more bold in terms of sharing my faith with people."

"Let's talk about what happened to you in 1970," Ted went on.

"I have Multiple Sclerosis," Tom said, gesturing toward his legs. "It's a disease of the central nervous system." This time the camera showed his whole body, including his wheelchair. "It affects people in different ways. In many people it tends to be progressive. But in my case, I went from walking with a slight limp in 1970, to using a wheelchair full-time in 1973. Since then my MS has been pretty stable."

"From 1970 to 1973, what was going on up here?" Ted asked, pointing to his head.

"I must confess that I asked God, 'Hey, how come this happened to me?' And God told me, in the way I think he talks to us, 'Who would you rather be?' After thinking about it, I realized there was nobody in the world I'd rather be than me.

"And then God said, 'What would you rather give up than your legs?' And I have to say that legs are one of the easiest things in the world to compensate for. I'd rather be unable to walk than unable to hear or see or speak or use my hands. I feel blessed that it's only my legs that have been affected."

As I listened to Tom's answer, I could feel the conviction in his voice. I couldn't have agreed with him more on that statement. I, too, felt really blessed that God had allowed me to recover as much as I had from my original paralysis.

Sure, there were times when it got really tough—and when physical exhaustion overwhelmed me. And yet I found that my attitude toward my circumstances depended so much on my life perspective. Just a year after graduating from Hamline University, I'd lived and worked in the Orient as a short-term medical missionary. And during my travels to and from Hong Kong, I had seen and heard of handicapped people who couldn't afford—or who didn't even have access to—the medical treatments and helpful equipment that are routinely available in the United States. Survival was the name of the game in most other countries. How could I ever complain about my circumstances?

"You used a phrase that tickled my fancy," Ted went on. "You said, 'God spoke to me in the way he does.' How does he?"

Tom smiled back at Ted and lifted his eyes heavenward. "Well, I believe that God speaks to us in a lot of different ways. In my case, he spoke to me through my trials with MS, by revealing things to me that I never believed possible before. I read the Bible a lot, and I also share with other people who in turn give me insights I'd never have thought of myself. And I see circumstances that lead me to make the best of a handicapped life. Now that's God saying to me, 'Hey Tom, you may be in a wheelchair, but you can do things you never imagined.' "

"And God gave you what you could handle. Is that right?" Mildred chimed in.

With a wide grin, Tom answered, "Praise the Lord! He promises not to test us beyond what we can bear. We have to be open to the way God wants to use our trials for his glory."

Tom's love for the Lord and his commitment to serving God in whatever way he could really shone through. *He certainly is bold in sharing his faith,* I thought. I liked that. In that way, Tom was a lot like my dad.

Then Ted interrupted, "Let's go back to that '70 to '73 period. Did you have a pretty hard time then?"

"Yes. I'm a bachelor, and it was tremendously difficult learning to cope with not being able to walk. I said if I couldn't walk I'd commit suicide."

Commit suicide! The words rang in my ears. My heart cried out, *Oh Tom, I'm so glad you didn't.* But I understood—without knowing the Lord, his life must have seemed utterly hopeless. I certainly knew that without God as the source of my strength, I could never live a victorious life as a handicapped individual.

"Then I felt the Lord telling me," Tom continued, "that the ballgame is never over until the last out. But it was still pretty hard. What got me through was not any strength of my own; it was the beautiful people God brought into my life. I have some of the greatest friends and family in the world. That's how I managed to get over some of the very difficult adjustment periods."

"So these people were some of the cogs in the wheel that turned Tom Carr around."

Tom nodded. "Recently I met a woman named Joni Eareckson, who has a wonderful ministry called Joni & Friends in the Woodland Hills area. She's a quadriplegic. Both of us recognize that we couldn't make it without our friends. Friends are really a key to overcoming our handicaps."

"Do you ever notice any resistance toward you because you're in a wheelchair?" Ted asked.

"I'd say it's probably just the opposite. Many people go out of their way to help me, to the point where they make me uncomfortable . . ."

"This disturbs you a little?"

"Just a little bit. I'd prefer they ask me first, before pushing me or trying to load my chair into the car. But that doesn't irritate me as much as seeing a non-handicapped person park in a handicap space."

Mildred spoke up again. "That bothers us a lot too. But I think it's getting better—probably because of the fines."

"As we draw this program to a close, do you have any recommendations for other handicapped people who might be watching here today?" Ted asked.

"I'd say to anyone who's physically handicapped, think about a career in engineering, because engineering tends to be a cerebral activity as opposed to a physical one. I can sit there and do my engineering job as well—maybe even better—than I could do it before I became handicapped. Computer programming is another good area."

"I've been deeply interested in your story, Tom, and in the faith that has been your sustaining backdrop through all the struggles you've faced."

"Ted, I would say that my faith, my family, and my friends are the most important elements of my life in overcoming MS."

"Thank you for being with us today. You've been an inspiration to us all!"

I beamed as I watched Tom being helped off the stage. I was so proud of him—and so thrilled to be able to share this experience with him. Maybe someday I, too, would earn a place in that group of caring friends Tom had talked about.

But deep in my heart, I hoped for more than that. I wanted to be the most special person in his life. Dare I even think the thought? *I wanted to be his wife.*

6

A Night to Remember

Tom

After the taping session, Ginny and I set out to find a spot for dinner. The interview had been far better than any I'd ever done before. Sharing my faith in Christ on a secular T.V. station had been an added bonus. I was in the mood to celebrate!

Ginny's company was another bonus. There had been many opportunities for special events in the past. But whether it was a Harvey Mudd College or MS Trustees dinner, an awards banquet, or another media presentation for Bechtel, I almost always went alone. It was great to have Ginny to share this exhilarating experience with. Earlier in the evening, I'd been anxious about being seen with a handicapped woman, but Ginny's sweetness seemed to put everyone, even me, at ease.

"Why don't we look for someplace on the Sunset Strip?" I suggested, looking over at Ginny. Her beaming countenance

revealed that this was already a never-to-be-forgotten evening for her, too. A fancy dinner would put a nice ending on
it for both of us. "Have you ever eaten in Hollywood
before?"

"I've been to Hollywood, but never for dinner. Isn't it
expensive?"

"It is, but don't worry—we'll find a place that I can afford."

We drove west, passing the Playboy Club, Perrino's,
Scandia, and the other top restaurants of Glitter City. The
sight of tuxedoed parking lot attendants warned me that
those places were probably out of my price range.

"Well, Ginny, I didn't see anything I could afford in Hollywood," I said, after we had driven beyond Restaurant
Row and were passing tall brick apartment buildings. "Why
don't we put the convertible top down and drive toward the
ocean? It's only a few minutes from here." I'd always loved
the ocean and looked forward to sharing it with someone
special. For tonight, Ginny was that someone.

"You did a great job, Tom," she said, as we cruised toward
the Pacific Coast Highway. "God has certainly given you an
ability to communicate."

I smiled back at her. "Last February I took a spiritual gifts
test. The results indicated that my greatest gifts are wisdom
and exhortation."

"Sounds like a pretty accurate test to me," she agreed.

"I enjoy encouraging people to make the most of their
lives. But the test also showed a third gift . . . celibacy."

Ginny's smile dissolved as I continued explaining. "I
know it's true. I haven't had a steady girlfriend in almost
four years. I used to date a lot before I became a Christian,

but now I'd rather stay home and read my Bible than go out on a random date."

Ginny stared straight ahead. *What was she thinking?* I wondered. *Would my remark slow down any romantic ideas she might be harboring?* Her childlike vitality was so refreshing it was disarming—and that scared me. Maybe that's why I'd blurted out those words about my gift of celibacy.

Suddenly the conversation was behind us, and we were over the top of a hill and catching our first glimpse of the Pacific. A breeze lifted Ginny's short brown hair, and the salty smell of sea air greeted us.

"Don't you love the ocean, Ginny?"

"I sure do. Almost every summer since I was a baby, our family spent vacations on the East Coast with my grandmother and uncle."

"When I lived in Manhattan Beach—before I got MS—I used to love to ride my bike or go walking along the shore. The air is so clean, and there's such a sense of freedom here. It's nice to get away from the city and relax, to listen to the sounds of the sea."

"I know what you mean. Our family would have hot dog roasts on the rocky Maine shoreline and sit for hours watching the pounding surf."

"Speaking of hot dogs, I'm starving. Let's see if we can pick one up here," I teased, turning into the parking lot of an elegant old English cottage style restaurant. The afterglow of the television interview and Ginny's radiant presence had transformed the evening into a serendipity not to be missed—no matter what the expense.

"Are your facilities wheelchair accessible?" I asked as the tuxedoed attendant approached.

"I don't know. Why don't you go in and find out?" he answered brusquely.

"Well, we're both handicapped," I replied, looking at the six stone steps leading up to the entryway. "Could you go in and ask if they have a wheelchair entrance?"

"Sorry, I'm the only one taking care of the parking lot," he said, turning toward an incoming car.

"Sorry about that, Ginny," I said, pulling back onto the highway. "It's probably not our kind of place anyway." I wanted a more hospitable spot to entertain her. The lack of proper markings regarding wheelchair access at restaurants and commercial businesses was a constant frustration and waste of time and energy.

I was embarrassed about taking her to a place that I couldn't even check out. Had the attendant seen my wheelchair and assumed it was for Ginny? It was a fairly normal response to expect the wheelchair user to be the passenger and not the driver. People were often amazed to learn that I could drive. And yet the modification required—a metal rod with a handle attached to the brake and accelerator, enabling me to drive with my hand—was surprisingly simple and inexpensive.

Less than a mile away, we found a white southern mansion-style restaurant, with a long wheelchair ramp on the outside of the building. We went in easily, used the spacious restrooms, and were seated graciously by the maitre d'. What a huge difference from the cold reception we'd received at our first stop!

"Didn't you say you'd spoken at a church in Burbank last Sunday?" Ginny asked, as the waiter placed a freshly brewed cup of coffee in front of her. "How did it go?"

"It went great. There were about three hundred people there to hear about Becky's healing—and mine."

"Yours?" Ginny asked with a puzzled look, as she lifted her coffee cup.

"Yes, mine. But first let me tell you about Becky's."

"O.K., but yours is the one I really want to hear about," Ginny said, smiling her ever-present, effervescent smile.

"Becky is a beautiful girl with big green eyes and long, blond hair. She was singing with a well-known vocal group back in 1969 when she developed Multiple Sclerosis. I met her in 1974 when we were co-chairpersons of the National Dance Marathon to raise funds for MS. We dated some, even though we were separated by almost a hundred freeway miles. She was the first handicapped girl I'd ever gotten to know well, and I felt she could really understand me, since she'd been crippled by MS too. We even joked about getting married someday."

As the waiter placed our salads on the table, I continued, "Do you know anyone who has MS?"

Ginny's expression grew serious. "The day I met you, I had lunch with Kathy, a friend who has MS. Her husband of six years had just left her."

"I've heard that story more than once. When MS—or any other disabling condition—hits, it can really destroy a family. I think people today have a 'I didn't marry a cripple' mentality. They fear that handicapped spouses will take too much time away from their careers and other things they want to do."

"Isn't it sad, Tom, that our society is so geared to good looks and healthy bodies? And yet Jesus taught that his strength could shine best through the lives of the weak."

"Vows of commitment, especially in the face of adversity, don't seem to mean much these days. But let's pray," I said, taking Ginny's hand.

"Dear Lord, this is not an easy world for anyone, but it can be especially hard for the handicapped. Thank you for allowing me to share my faith today; we pray that it will be an encouragement to many. Bless the rest of the evening and the food. In Jesus' holy name, amen. Oh—and please make it non-fattening!"

"That was beautiful, Tom."

"It's been quite an evening." I squeezed her hand one last time. "That is, unless I starve to death. Let's eat."

"Except for Kathy and two other women," Ginny went on as she passed me the basket of warm bread, "I really don't know anyone else with MS. And I don't know much about it either."

"Well, if you're looking for information, you came to the right guy," I said, jumping at the chance to do a little bragging. "I just happen to be a trustee of the Southern California chapter of the National Multiple Sclerosis Society. Would you like to hear my 60-second PR speech?"

"Sure. I want to understand everything I can."

"MS is called the disease of the young, the strong, and the beautiful. It mainly attacks adults between eighteen and forty—about sixty percent of them are women. I was hit at twenty-three. The myelin sheath—the protective insulation around the nerves—becomes so inflamed that messages from the brain to the muscles are impaired or blocked. There is no known cause or cure."

"It sounds bad—frightening," she said.

"For me, it was mainly an inconvenience at first—poor balance, a little double vision in the summer, incontinence . . . Do you know what incontinence is?"

"Of course—lack of bladder control. I'm a med tech, remember?"

"I'm sorry. How could I forget? Anyway, by 1973, I had an indwelling catheter and was in a wheelchair full-time. But you know what? This wheelchair brought me out of the deep depression that trying to hobble around had caused me. It's been a great blessing."

"I'm glad," Ginny said, with a look of understanding in her eyes.

"MS is usually a progressively disabling disease, though some people have remissions and the disease can tend to stabilize somewhat. Becky's condition seemed just like mine when I first met her."

"You mean she used a wheelchair?" Ginny asked.

"Yes, and a catheter."

"How did you ever date her with two chairs to worry about?"

"It wasn't easy. Just imagine, when we went to the movie 'The Other Side of the Mountain,' there we were—two people who couldn't stand or walk—trying to put two chairs in the back of my Mustang."

"How did you do it?"

"I'm not sure. Just dogged determination, I guess. It took almost ten minutes, and we laughed at how silly we must have looked."

"At least you could laugh about it. You really have a great sense of humor, Tom."

"I'm sure you know how discouraging a handicap can be, Ginny. You just have to keep a positive attitude."

"You're right about that! But what about Becky?"

"In 1976, she went downhill fast, losing even the ability to use her hands. When I visited her at the hospital, she couldn't move a muscle on her torso."

"What a severe case!"

"That's the way MS can be. It's an unpredictable disease—you can feel good one day and be paralyzed the next. But Becky just lay there in her hospital bed praising the Lord."

"Talk about a calm in the midst of the storm. What faith."

"Mountain-moving faith, Ginny," I said, looking directly into her listening eyes. "Seeing her faith in God, despite her circumstances, had a profound impact on me. Then Becky recovered slightly and flew to San Francisco to visit her cousin and her family. While she was there, they prayed for her healing.

"In the twinkling of an eye, she was totally healed. She got out of bed, walked outside, and rode her nephew's bicycle. She could move just like she had before MS—as if nothing had ever been wrong." Ginny sat mesmerized, looking intently at me as I continued the story.

"When she got home to Los Angeles, her doctor was astonished as he watched her walk through the hospital lobby. He pointed out that her problems with MS were especially severe and that it was highly unusual for someone who had been paralyzed and unable to walk for seven years to be up and around all of a sudden. He's convinced it was a miracle from the Lord, and now he's given her a clean bill of health."

"Wow—I can hardly believe it," Ginny exclaimed, staring incredulously at me. "She is totally healed? Nothing remains of the MS?"

"As far as I know. She was well enough to push me around Dodger Stadium last summer."

"That's incredible! But what about you? You said something about your own healing," Ginny said eagerly, as the waiter took away our salad plates.

"Have you ever had anybody pray for you to be healed, Ginny?"

"Once, when I was young. But nothing happened. It was wonderful of them to pray for my healing, but at the time I really didn't understand it. I thought I was okay just the way I was."

Truly, as I looked across the table at Ginny, there was no visible evidence of any handicap. Although I knew there was a metal leg brace and two wooden crutches somewhere under the white linen tablecloth, Ginny didn't appear limited at all. Her fashionable dress showcased her beauty and femininity. And her glowing smile testified to a healthier attitude about life than most people I knew.

"I've been prayed over many times, too. A few years ago, a group of people at a convention prayed for me. Although I didn't get up and walk that night, they assured me I'd be healed if I returned the next evening."

"Did you go back?"

"No, but I did turn on the local Christian television station to watch the closing program the next night. Pat Robertson spoke, closing with a challenge for those listening to confess their sins and give their lives to Christ.

"Before I became a Christian, I'd done a lot of drinking and running around with women—and I still had animosity toward others. I knew I could never earn God's forgiveness for my sins. But when I heard him say that God's gift of forgiveness and eternal life was free, I decided to accept it and invite Jesus into my life. Suddenly I felt an overwhelming sense of God's presence."

"Isn't it incredible," Ginny interrupted, "that the God of the universe cares about us? It's so simple, so easy. All it takes is a childlike faith . . ."

"But a scientist can believe it, too," I added. "When I used to wonder about where the world came from, I'd hear people claim that it just evolved. That required a greater leap of faith than believing in biblical creation. The probability that the natural order of the universe could have 'just happened' is preposterous."

"Being a microbiologist, I know what you mean," Ginny responded. "Every time I look under my microscope and observe the intricacies of life, it makes me feel closer to God than ever."

"That's right, but it still takes faith—not just intellect," I agreed, realizing that my spiritual healing was far more important to Ginny than any physical one I might receive. "I remember Billy Graham explaining how he used faith constantly in daily life. For example, he didn't know why a brown cow could eat green grass and yield white milk, but he still drank milk."

"And yet so many people fail to recognize the Lord," Ginny said, shaking her head.

"I still don't understand everything about God, but I can't doubt that he's real. I think it was the philosopher Pascal who said there is a God-shaped vacuum in every heart. I've asked God to fill mine."

While the waiter placed our entrees—fresh broiled halibut for Ginny and an end cut of prime rib for me—on the table, Ginny continued. "So you're saying your healing wasn't physical, it was spiritual?"

"The story doesn't end there. My physical healing began back in February of this year after a total stranger left a note

on my door saying God had told him to take me to a Mario
Murillo Miracle Service in Pasadena."

"A total stranger? What did you do?"

"I prayed about it, and listened as another stranger inde-
pendently recommended that I attend. So I went."

"With strangers?"

"The first guy had met me once at my condo. He said the
wheelchair bag I had at the time, embroidered with the
words "God Loves You, and So Do I," had inspired him to
investigate Christianity. He later accepted Christ as his
Savior. The second guy was at a breakfast meeting I'd been
to that morning, so they were both brothers in the Lord."

"And what happened?"

"After Mario preached, he prayed for people to be healed.
I saw several people come up on the platform and announce
that they'd been healed of things like diabetes and hemorrhoids."

"How can you verify something like that?" Ginny asked.

"Exactly my thinking, too. But when I saw a husky man
carrying two small, metal leg braces, my skepticism
evaporated. Right beside him ambled a smiling little boy
with dark brown tousled hair—he looked about five years
old. The father was sobbing as he stepped up to the
microphone and explained that his son had been born with
a congenital hip displacement and had never been able to
walk without his braces before. But now God had healed
him."

Ginny put her fork down and stared at me. "Wow. What
did you think of that?"

"I was impressed. That little boy was a miracle! His healing was real, even though I didn't receive mine.

"Then, when Mario started to pray again, about half a
dozen men and women surrounded me. They began im-
ploring me to get up, saying, 'You're healed. Try to stand.

Just have more faith. You've got to believe. Confess your sins and let God heal you.' They practically demanded that I rise and walk."

"What did you do then?"

"I truly wanted to get up, but when I tried to make my legs straighten out and stand, they buckled and threw me back on the arm of the chair."

Ginny's eyes filled with compassion as she reached over to put her hand on mine.

"Then I heard the Lord speaking to my spirit in a soft, gentle whisper. *You've been healed, Tom, but faith is the substance of things hoped for and the evidence of things not seen.*

"I recognized Hebrews 11:1 as the message God was revealing to me. I hadn't really believed that God was the healer of diabetes or hemorrhoids. But now I was expecting my legs to be restored? I felt God telling me that my healing was real, but like a woman's pregnancy, it would not begin to show physically for several months. From that day four months ago, I have absolutely believed I've been healed. It's just a question of when—and how he shows it."

"What do your friends think about it?"

"I've only told the guys in my Bible study group. We're all praying that I'll be walking by Christmas. But I would appreciate your prayers for me, too."

7

A Long Lost Love

Tom

Rustic wrought-iron lanterns cast a warm glow over La Fiesta's walls, hung with old ponchos, sombreros, and clay pots. It had a simple south-of-the-border atmosphere, but Ginny's wide-eyed look as we entered confirmed what she'd told me on our first date. Eating in a nice restaurant was a wonderful change from her usual after work "drive-thru" routine.

"Thanks for inviting me to have dinner with you," she said, as a short-skirted señorita brought her a cup of coffee and took our order.

"Hey, I'm the one who should be thanking you," I replied, as a dark-haired waiter placed a basket of taco chips and green salsa in front of us. "I hope it's not going to be too late by the time you get back from the airport. My plane doesn't leave until ten o'clock."

"Oh, don't worry. I'll be fine, but I'll miss you."

Ginny's words caught me off-guard. We'd known each other for less than a month, but already I sensed that my friendship was an important part of her world. And yet she knew so little about the real me, about the loose-living past I was trying to forget. Perhaps I should have driven myself to the airport and avoided fostering this relationship.

"Where did you say you're going, Tom?"

"To Orlando to see my mother and then on to Chicago for an energy conference."

"When did you last see your mom?"

"How does sixteen years sound? At my high school graduation in 1964," I said, trying to sound indifferent.

"What happened?" she probed, a surprised and perplexed look replacing her smile. "Why so long?"

I picked at the shredded lettuce piled high on my tostada, then took a deep breath and looked away. "It's a complicated story, Ginny. I'll tell you about it when I get back."

Two hours later, I boarded the airplane and collapsed, exhausted, into my seat. Was it the long workday and the late drive to the airport that had done me in? Or was it the excitement—and anxiety—I felt over being with my mother for the first time as an adult? Thoughts of what might lie ahead kept me awake almost the whole flight to Orlando.

As sleep eluded me, my mind flashed back to a crisp winter evening last December. I'd been sitting at my oak desk, pondering the words on the application form in front of me: MOTHER'S NAME. I was applying for a North American Ministerial Fellowship to go to seminary. Although I'd filled out applications for everything from credit cards to automobile loans to health insurance, never had a question seemed so difficult. It looked simple enough— MOTHER'S NAME—but I was stumped for an answer. My head said "Phyllis Carr," but my heart declared "not applicable."

If anyone could claim that his mother was "not applicable," certainly I could. My parents separated when I was only ten months old, and I'd been sent to live with my dad's brother and his family while the divorce was being settled. When I was seven, my dad finally brought me to live with him and my teenaged sister and brother. I cried and cried on the day I had to leave my Aunt Hazel. She was the only mom I'd ever known.

As I progressed from grade school to junior high, my sister Jane became "mom" to me. She cooked delicious spare ribs and mashed potatoes, tucked me into bed at night, and seldom scolded me without pointing out, "I still love you, Tom, but I don't like what you did!" Jane took me to Sunday school and gave me my first Bible. She was everything I thought a mom should be. I seldom saw my real mom, and nobody but my brother, Jim—he'd lived with her for several years during the divorce proceedings—ever said anything about her. Since she'd never been a part of my life, I felt totally indifferent toward her.

The only time I remembered seeing her as a youth was in 1964, when Jim asked me to invite her to my high school graduation. He felt she'd enjoy coming, so I invited her. Although she traveled from her home in Florida for my graduation (and stayed in the area for the summer), I was too busy to spend any time with "Jim's mother." I was doing just fine without a mother, and I didn't need her complicating my life.

Until 1976, I really hadn't thought of her again. Then, as a young Christian, I applied for a seminary fellowship, answering the "Mother's Name" question with "divorced."

I won the scholarship, but—in light of my MS condition—chose not to risk leaving my good-paying job and generous medical benefits for the ministry.

As my faith and trust in God grew during the next three years, a term paper I'd written as a seventh grader—about my dream to become a minister—began to haunt me. I decided to apply for the fellowship again.

As I was filling out the application this time, however, I realized I couldn't possibly become a leader of the family of God when I considered my own mother "not applicable." I would have to restore my relationship with her.

On Christmas Day, I called my brother in Buffalo. "Jim, I want your mother's address."

"What did you say?"

"I want to write to our mom," I corrected myself, calling her "Mom" for the first time in my life.

"That would be the greatest Christmas present she's ever received," Jim replied, reciting her address and phone number from memory.

For two weeks the address collected dust on my desk. Then one night, as I started to slide into bed, I froze, realizing that I had to contact her. It was midnight, but I knew I wouldn't be able to sleep until I wrote her that long overdue letter.

The words came slowly, each sentence more difficult than the previous one. I was afraid she'd confront me or ask for money, but I had to risk it.

"I'm sorry I've never written you, Mom . . ." I began. " . . . Maybe we can have a relationship like you and Jim have someday."

It was a brief letter, but I was exhausted when I finished it. Why, and how, does a thirty-three-year-old man reach out to a mother he has ignored for years? I had no idea, except that God's Word required me to do it.

Ten days later I pulled two envelopes from my mailbox. One was from the North American Ministerial Fellowship Committee. I ripped it open and scanned its contents.

"Thank you for your application . . . We received many . . . Yours will not be advanced to the finals."

No reason was given for the rejection. It was just a tough-luck-but-you-didn't-make-it form letter. I couldn't believe my eyes. Since I'd won the fellowship three years ago, my career had progressed, my references were more supportive, and my commitment to ministry was stronger than ever. What had gone wrong?

Crushed, I dropped the letter to the floor and reached for the second one. It was from my mom.

"Tom, my joy knows no bounds. It seems that I have prayed a lifetime for your letter. I forgive you. We can and will build a relationship."

I read the words over again. "My joy knows no bounds!" Instantly, her letter lifted a tremendous burden of unforgiveness and neglect from my heart. I had just discovered my mother for the first time in my life. The fellowship application didn't seem so important anymore.

On Saturday I phoned her. "Tom, I'd know your voice in a minute," she cried. "A mother always knows her children. Write and tell me all about yourself. How's your health? Jimmy told me that you have Multiple Sclerosis. Is there anything I can do to help? I love you."

When I hung up the phone, my head was spinning. How could she act like she'd known me all my life? She'd hardly ever seen or talked to me. I was scared that she'd want to come and "take care of me," that she'd want to be more than a long-distance friend. I couldn't understand my feelings or hers, but I felt that a new relationship was beginning to grow.

For the next four months, the letters flew between California and Florida. Mom was monetarily poor but proud of how she'd managed. She'd even been to Europe twice, while I'd never gone beyond the border towns of Canada and Mexico. It would be wonderful to meet and get to know this woman—my mother.

"Fasten your seatbelts please," the captain announced in a deep voice, arousing me from my musings and memories. "The time is 8:05 A.M., eastern daylight time. Orlando, Florida welcomes you to the home of Disneyworld and the EPCOT Center."

As the plane touched down, my heart began to pound in my chest. Like a championship tennis match before the first ball is hit, the tension was enormous.

After the other passengers had exited, a flight attendant helped me into my wheelchair and rolled me toward the lounge. There were hoards of people milling around and checking baggage for the next flight. *Will I even recognize my own mother?* I wondered.

Then I saw her standing at the back of the lounge. There was no doubt she was my mother. Although her wrinkles and graying hair declared she was a senior citizen, her decisive stride as she moved through the jostling crowd denied it. I wanted to leap out of my wheelchair and run to her arms.

"Mom!" I shouted across the room, as the flight attendant attempted to navigate me toward the back.

Finally, we met and embraced for the first time ever, separated only by the steel bars of my wheelchair. "Son, it's so great that you've finally come to see me," she said, as we hugged for a moment. The lost love between us, the love that had been building for the past six months, was finally being set free.

"I've been waiting so long for this moment, Tom," she said softly, kissing me as a tear rolled down her cheek. "I sure am blessed to have two handsome sons like you and Jimmy." I wondered how she could feel that way when I had ignored her for so many years. I could hardly believe it; we were finally together!

On the drive to her house, Mom asked, with a twinkle in her eye, "Tell me about yourself, sweetheart. I know you'll be thirty-four next week. Are you planning to be a committed bachelor like your brother? There *are* girls in California, aren't there?"

"Sure. And I've dated a lot in the past. But I'm really not that interested anymore. I've struck up a friendship with a handicapped girl, but my career's the big thing now," I explained, changing the subject.

Over dinner the following evening, at an old seafood shanty, we continued to get to know each other.

"What made you finally write me?" she asked.

"My conscience has been gnawing at me ever since Dad died four years ago. I was sorry that I hadn't been close to him—at best we'd been roommates. And I wish I'd told him how much I appreciated his hard work to provide for us.

"Then one evening as I read my Bible, I was convicted by Matthew 15:6, which says not to give tithes to the church if your parents are in need. I knew it was too late to help Dad, but I could still help you."

"I'm so thankful you've seen the light, son," she said, her face brightening.

I squeezed her hand. "But, Mom, why didn't *you* ever come to see me?"

"Oh Tom, I tried so hard to see you. But your dad wouldn't let me. Finally I gave up. I knew all I could do was pray." My heart melted at the thought that she had wanted to see me all these years.

We spent the next day at Disneyworld. While we sat on a terrace overlooking the lush tropical gardens, listening to birds chirping all around us, I couldn't help thinking of the home we'd return to in the evening. Mom's house had a leaky roof and plumbing that worked only once every hour. It had no air conditioning. Her bathroom wasn't even large enough for my wheelchair.

Mom had mentioned her dream of selling the house and buying a nice mobile home to live in. It seemed like a well-deserved dream. Although I didn't know where I'd get the money, I determined to help her buy it.

"Mom, if you could have anything in the world, what would you wish for?"

She hesitated for a moment. "Just that you'd be well, son!" she replied softly, patting my hand.

"Oh, Mom," I sobbed. I was stunned that she didn't want material things, but instead was more interested in my health. Tears rolled down my face as I realized how different she was from the woman I had feared to know. "I'd give you anything, Mom, but only God can restore my health."

"I prayed for all these years that you'd accept me as your mother. Now I'm going to pray that you'll be well," she told me, wiping the moisture from her cheeks. "Then my wish will come true."

"Mom, I believe God has promised me just that. Keep praying," I implored her.

The next afternoon as I kissed her good-bye and boarded the plane for Chicago, I reflected on the love that my newly-discovered mom had for me. It had been there all the time.

All I had to do was to reach out and receive it. It was like that with God, too. Until I made the conscious decision to reach out to him and take that first step, I never knew how close he was. He was just waiting for me to acknowledge his presence and ask his forgiveness for my sins, so he could wrap me in his infinite love.

I knew now that the restoring of my relationship with Mom had to take place before God could bring any physical healing into my life. But with both of us praying, I believed that my healing was destined to happen.

8
Falling in Like

Ginny

T*he lazy, hazy, crazy days of summer,* I mused, as I drove down Imperial Highway. My summers usually weren't all that exciting, but this one was off to a great start!

Tom was back from his trip, and we both had the day off, so he'd invited me to join him for an afternoon swim at his condo. What a treat on this hot July afternoon.

Tracing the route to his place, I reflected on our drive home from the airport last night. Finally he had filled me in on the details of his perplexing relationship with his mother. Although he'd told me what wonderful moms his Aunt Hazel and his sister had been, I couldn't imagine growing up without a real mother. My own mother had played such a significant role in my childhood. I especially remembered her love in action—many a night she stayed up late to finish sewing new outfits for me. And even though she worked as a nurse to help make ends meet, she always seemed to be there when I needed her.

I was glad Tom had finally reconciled with his mom. Life was too short to hold a grudge against a family member—or anyone, for that matter.

Arriving at Tom's condo, I parked my car and walked the paved pathway leading to the pool. The sweet scent of star-like blooming plumaria filled the air, and I marveled at the beauty of the lush green foliage. A forest of ferns and tall pines surrounded me, and a stream meandered lazily under a small footbridge. To the left a waterfall splashed over some large boulders. *What an incredible place to live,* I thought.

"Hi, Ginny," Tom called out as soon as he spotted me. His tanned chest glistened in the sun as he sat half submerged on the pool steps, catching his breath. "Come on in. The water's great!" he said, plunging under for another lap.

He had told me that swimming was his favorite type of exercise; one of the few, as a handicapped person, he could do well. I loved to swim too. A college student who attended our church had taught me to swim when I was in the fourth grade. But I'd never lived near a pool, so I rarely had the opportunity. I hoped this would be an activity—other than eating—that Tom and I could enjoy together.

As I removed my beach top I noticed that the bright sunlight made my blue one-piece swimsuit look a bit worn and faded. Since I couldn't go to Maine with my family in August, I hadn't expected to swim at all this season. *I'll have to get a new suit, but it's too late now,* I thought, as I sat down at the edge of the pool to remove my leg brace.

Chuckling, I told Tom, "Little kids are always asking me, 'Can you take that thing off? Can you swim with that on?' Or 'Do you wear that to bed?' "

"They've always got plenty of questions for me too," he laughed. He was still trying to catch his breath as he went on. "Hot days like this are hard on people who have MS.

About ten to fifteen minutes in this sun, and I'm done for. Unless I can fall into the pool, that is."

"So you really have to be careful in the summer?"

"Right. On hot summer days I've got to be in an air-conditioned building or in a pool cooling off. Otherwise the heat makes my body go limp as a dishrag until I can get cooled off again." He looked up at the blazing sun. "Prolonged exposure to heat can even cause MS to get permanently worse."

"I didn't know that."

"Yeah, sometimes it makes me sad. I used to love the summertime, but now the heat is too hard on me."

This was the first hint of discouragement I'd heard in his voice since the day I met him. He was always so upbeat and seemed to be so well adjusted to his limitations. Having had polio at such a young age, I'd grown up never really knowing what I had missed. But it was different for Tom. He had been so athletic.

"Let's get with it," he said, splashing me with cold water and dropping from the step back into the pool. "Let's race."

"How far?" I asked, eyeing the deep end about fifty feet away.

"Ten lengths," he replied. "That should take about seven or eight minutes. Ready, get . . ."

"Hey, wait a minute. I don't think I can swim that many."

"What do you mean? I do it all the time, and you've got one more leg to kick with than I do. Go," he shouted as he plunged under the water.

I raced after him, propelling myself with my strong arms and my one good leg. The water was a place where we could both feel free and less encumbered by our handicaps. After five lengths, I stopped at the deep end, holding on as Tom arrived a stroke or two later.

"Hey, you can't stop . . .," he gurgled out between breaths as he bobbed in the water. "We're only halfway, and the second half's always my best."

"That's not fair. Let's stop for a minute."

"Well, loser buys dinner," he announced, plunging under again before I could say anything else. I watched as his muscular upper body propelled him under the water in a breaststroke. His legs partly floated and partly dragged behind. He stayed under all the way, then turned and started back, using the backstroke. His strokes showcased his determination as he fought the deadweight downward pull of his legs. It was obvious he wasn't going to let his handicap stop him.

"Tough luck—you're buying, Ginny," he declared, pulling himself over to the side. "I think I'm in the mood for French food. How would you like to take me to Chez Cary?"

"Okay. Where's that?" I asked, wondering if I'd need to go home and change clothes.

He laughed. "I'm just kidding, Ginny. Chez Cary is about the fanciest and most expensive restaurant in Orange County. Let's just relax for a while. Then we'll go over to the mall and have dinner."

Several hours later two young guys who had been playing a game of chess out by the pool helped Tom into his wheelchair. Then we changed into street clothes and drove up the block to a New Orleans style café. We picked a table in the open patio area at the front of the restaurant, overlooking the main mall walkway.

"Coffee?" the waitress asked as she came by our table. The aroma of freshly roasted coffee beans wafted through the air. How could I resist?

"Yes, please," I responded enthusiastically.

Tom looked up at the waitress. "Not for me, thanks, but you know these Scandanavians—they can't live without their coffee," he said, winking at me.

We chatted leisurely and watched the people stroll by. I had learned to enjoy "people watching" during my childhood. Often, when the rest of the family and friends were off combing the beach or climbing over rocks near the ocean, I could remember my mother saying, "Virginia, why don't you and I sit here, rest awhile, and watch the people go by." We'd see all shapes and sizes of humanity and try to imagine who they were and where they were going. Those were special times we had together—just my mom and me. I was glad to be sharing similar moments with this special man.

I watched as two tall, shapely, sun-tanned blondes in shorts and tank tops walked by us. Tom watched too. From various things I'd picked up in our conversations, it seemed that Tom had a lot of girls as friends. He'd told me that recently he had taken the nurse from his doctor's office out to dinner. And next weekend he wanted me to meet a gal who'd be visiting from the San Francisco area. I didn't know if that was a good sign or not. In the time we'd known each other I hadn't met a single one of his friends. Was this girl just a casual acquaintance—or was she part of the competition? From one day to the next, I didn't know if I'd ever see Tom again.

As the waitress refilled my coffee cup and took our orders, Tom asked, "Ginny, do you have brothers or sisters? I've told you all about my family, but I don't know anything about yours."

"My sister, Marylin, lives in Wheaton, Illinois with her husband and two children. She was a homecoming queen too, in her senior year at Trinity College. I was so happy for her."

"Incredible! Two queens in one family. I bet your parents were proud."

"They sure were! I also have a brother, Dave, who lives in Milwaukee. Both Dave and Marylin are very special to me."

"And you're a long way from them. You must miss your family."

"I do, but even though we don't get to see one another nearly as much as we'd like, I still feel very close to them."

The waitress interrupted us to place our spicy chicken and vegetable entrees and fresh apple fritters on the table. Then Tom continued, "You haven't mentioned it, Ginny, but wasn't it hard growing up with a handicap?"

I helped myself to one of the piping hot apple fritters and passed them over to Tom. "At times. But if my parents hadn't modeled such a strong faith in God, it would have been even more difficult."

"What do you mean by that?"

I paused to think for a moment. "They helped me learn to deal with my trials, but encouraged me not to dwell on them. By their example, they taught me to focus on the Lord and to trust him to bring me through hardships."

"Your smile certainly shows that you're a victor—not a victim—of polio."

I grinned back at him. "My dad set a great example for me. When he was twelve years old, he had a serious injury— his ankle was crushed in a combine on the family farm. He walked with a leg brace and crutches for almost six years himself, but he never let his injury stop him from being a hard worker and a great father. His enthusiasm and determination inspired me to do my best too."

"With a family like that, no wonder you've got such a positive outlook."

I nodded. "My family played an invaluable role in helping me rise above my disability. I can remember my mother reading 'The Little Engine That Could' to me when I was a little girl. It was my favorite!

"And my parents taught me early that Jesus was my friend, that he loved me and had a unique plan for my life. I've learned that God doesn't make mistakes in what he allows. God has used adverse circumstances to make me strong, to make me into the person he wants me to be."

Tom's expression grew tender, as he looked into my eyes. His gaze was so direct that I felt I was melting inside.

"Ginny," he said softly, "you are such a beautiful person and so much fun to be with. I—I think I might be falling in love with you."

I could hardly believe my ears! My heart pounded, and I felt weak all over. These were the words I'd been waiting all my life to hear. I'd prayed that God would only let the *right* guy fall in love with me. Was Tom the one? Was this really happening?

"Oh, Tom, I'm so glad . . ." I whispered, gazing back at him. "I know I love you."

Tom held my hand in his, caressing it gently. For that moment in time, we were alone in a private world. I wanted to stay there forever.

After finishing our dinner, we headed back toward the car. As I walked along beside Tom's wheelchair, my heart skipped joyfully. People looked at us curiously—they probably wondered how two handicapped people could be so happy!

Then as Tom slid out of his wheelchair and into the car, his tone grew solemn. "Ginny, I've been thinking about what I said over dinner."

"About what?" My heart sank. *Now what?*

"Well, that I might be falling in love with you. For now, anyway, I better change it to falling in 'like' with you."

A lump swelled in my throat, and I stared back at him. I knew it had been too good to be true. I wanted so much to have someone to love and to care about. *At least my abandoned kittens love me*, I thought.

He went on slowly. "My career is really on a roll right now. I'm doing a lot of traveling and the B-E-S-T—that's short for Bechtel Energy Speakers Team—the group which I'm in charge of, gave over 250 speeches this year. I'm also writing a USC (University of Southern California) course for Mr. Caraco, my boss, to teach . . . There are a lot of great things happening."

"How does all that affect me?" I asked, torn between puzzlement and depression.

"Ginny, I'm just too busy to think about falling in love with anyone."

He is so in love with his job! I thought. My spirits plummeted, and I felt sick inside. Tom and I always had such fun until he started analyzing everything. Then his head and his heart just couldn't seem to agree.

From that moment on, I resolved to think of Tom—and to speak of him—only as a good friend, even though my heart felt so much more. I had to protect myself! That way, if things didn't work out for us, I wouldn't have to explain anything—to anyone.

Was it just wishful thinking to imagine that a man might fall in love with me?

"But I'll make you an offer, Ginny. I'll give you a three-month friendship contract," Tom said.

"What's a friendship contract?" I asked, a hint of irritation in my voice. I'd never heard of such a thing. *How businesslike!* I thought.

"We'll go places and be friends through the summer," he responded softly, touching my shoulder. "Then we'll re-evaluate things and see where we go from there."

We sat there with the convertible top down, bathed in a travelogue California night. Again I wondered, *Am I winning or losing my dream?* Maybe this contract thing was just a way for Tom to get out of our friendship with no regrets.

Do I really need this? my heart asked.

9

What Am I Afraid Of?

Tom

"Happy Birthday to you, Happy Birthday to you," the feminine voice on the other end of the telephone line sang out. My heart skipped a beat—it was Pam. I hadn't talked to her since the concert in April.

"It's nice of you to remember, Pam," I said.

"Well, I've got a surprise for you. How would you like us to take you out to dinner?"

"Us? Who's us?"

"Suzanne and I. You helped each of us celebrate our birthday and we want to take you to a dinner-theater for yours," Pam said, with an air of anticipation in her voice.

"Wow! Such a deal! That's an irresistible package—two of my favorite girls, a free meal, and a show to boot. Where and when?"

"We'll pick you up at five on Sunday, and then we'll tell you where. Dress California-casual, and bring your best appetite because the food's going to be scrumptious and abundant!"

I smiled as I hung up the phone. I was glad Pam had called. We were great friends, but I had initiated all our meetings or phone calls until now. Perhaps that poem I wrote for her thirtieth birthday had touched her heart after all. And I was glad I had amended my remarks to Ginny earlier this week. Certainly our "friendship contract" was not compromised if I spent time with Pam.

I was excited when Pam and Suzanne arrived on Sunday. They were both beautiful women. Although Suzanne with her long, blonde hair was more striking, Pam's girl-next-door looks appealed more to me. Her short, brown hair and flawless complexion made her the All-American girl I'd always wanted to date. Pam met almost all my criteria. She was attractive, intelligent, and she loved the Lord.

"Do you want to drive or should I?" I asked, as we left my condo and headed for the parking lot, eyeing Pam's little red Datsun.

"I'll drive, if you think we can get your chair in," Pam answered, taking her keys out of her purse.

"It'll probably be more comfortable than trying to squeeze you both into the passenger seat of my Mustang!" The back seat had been removed to make space for my wheelchair.

The thought of me—a guy in a wheelchair—being seen with two good-looking women—was a neat one. Back in my Manhattan Beach days, appearances were everything. Great looks, well-tanned muscular bodies, fancy clothes, and sleek sport cars were always "in." Now that I was a Christian, impressing people wasn't so important to me anymore, but it still felt good to think people would be impressed by my date—or dates!

At the dinner-theater, the girls grimaced when they saw three steps leading up to the entrance and no ramp. They weren't strong enough to transport a 170-pound man and a forty-pound wheelchair up those steps.

"What do we do now, Tom?" Pam asked.

"Go to the box office and ask if there's a back entrance. Most older places bring the wheelchairs in through the kitchen—with the meat and potato deliveries," I laughed.

"Don't they have laws requiring accessibility?" Pam asked.

"Well, the Rehabilitation Act of 1973 requires all new buildings, including those being renovated, to provide a wheelchair entrance, elevators to other floors and access to restrooms," I replied, getting on my soapbox for a moment. It was sometimes humiliating—and downright uncomfortable—to sit at a back door ringing a buzzer which might not even be working.

Pam went up to the box office and the manager came out quickly to take me around to the kitchen door. I rolled past trays of vegetables—bright orange carrots, big red radishes, green chili peppers. This would undoubtedly be my only chance to check out the selection, since buffet aisles were rarely wide enough for wheelchairs.

"Tom, do you want us to get you a plate?" Pam asked, as they called our table to the buffet.

"That'll be great. Get me a little bit of everything they've got. I'm really hungry tonight."

"You always are. You eat up a storm every time I see you, yet you never put on any weight."

"Well, that's what it's like being a bachelor. You only eat when someone else is doing the cooking," I said, winking at

Suzanne. "Half the time you're starving, and half the time you're stuffed. If I ate two or three meals a day, I'd probably look like an army tank rolling down the street." They both laughed, then headed toward the buffet line.

The auditorium was tiered with about fifteen rows of tables, ten people squeezed together at each. We had been strategically placed in the first row on the right side of the stage. My wheelchair tires were almost touching a set of stage lights—top-dollar seats.

After dinner, the lights dimmed and the curtain went up. The play was a comedy, "Chapter Two," by Neil Simon. Pam, the girl of my dreams—or so I thought—quickly became engrossed in the play and never looked my way. I watched her out of the corner of my eye as she smiled and laughed at the comedic situations. I hoped she would look over at me at some tender moment in the play and give me a loving glance. But whenever she did look my way, it was with a weak smile at best.

The play's heroine, Jenny, had a sweet, loving nature. As the play continued, she kept reminding me of Ginny. *How ironic*, I thought, *that even their names sound alike*. If I hadn't read the program, I would have thought the other actors were calling her "Ginny."

When the lights dimmed for the last scene—a poignant one between Jenny and the male lead, George—I looked over at Pam again. She never even glanced in my direction. I had thought God might use this evening to spark a romance, but now I was wondering if this was the end, rather than the beginning, of any romantic relationship.

Suddenly, the sound of George's voice drew me back into the drama. ". . . and I remembered a question Dr. Ornstein, my psychiatrist, told me to ask myself whenever I felt trouble coming on. 'George, what is it you're most afraid would happen if . . .?' " Then George finished the question by adding "if I went back to Jenny?"

His words hit me hard. Although they were spoken by an actor in a play, they seemed to fit my own situation so well. I thought of the heroine, Jenny, and how she couldn't understand George's reluctance to return her affection. And I wondered what was keeping Pam from loving me. I knew she had great respect for me as a Christian, a communicator, and a friend. But we had never shared the warmth of a close personal relationship.

Then I heard George whisper his reply, "I would be happy."

Those words shook me. I looked over at Pam as she stared at the stage. I had no idea if I could really make her, or any other woman for that matter, happy.

Except Ginny! She seemed to appreciate even the smallest things I did for her—like bringing her a bouquet of carnations or taking her out for a simple dinner. A feeling of warmth flooded over me as I thought about her happy, loving nature.

I looked back at Pam. Her qualities—beauty, intelligence, and spirituality—were great. But so were Ginny's! And Ginny was clearly more interested in me. Certainly, none of the other girls I'd dated had ever treated me as warmly as she did.

Could it be, I wondered, *that what God has in mind for me is a lot different than what I have been dreaming of?* Maybe this play wasn't a scenario about Pam not loving me—perhaps it was about me being afraid to love Ginny.

That "three-month contract" was sounding better all the time!

10

The Walls Begin to Crumble

Tom

Exciting—that's the only way to describe the summer which was streaking by at a record pace. It was only the middle of July, but my calendar already overflowed with great potential.

Let's see, I thought, as I sat at my dining room table, flipping through my daytimer. Angels game with the men's fellowship from Anaheim Hills Community Church, MS Trustees meeting, two Bechtel speeches, preview showing of the new "Joni" film . . .

The new "Joni" film—being in charge of North Orange County publicity was going to be a big job. I'd have to find someone to help. Then I saw the next date. "Ginny Holty—dinner/theater—her treat." I flipped back through my calendar. Yes, Ginny had more spots than Bechtel speeches and other activities combined. It didn't surprise me. She was so much fun to be with.

She might be a good candidate for co-chair of the "Joni" film. After all, she was a deaconness at the Fullerton Free Church. Just getting each of the 5,000 people who attended there on Sunday to go and bring a friend would guarantee a week of movie theater sellouts.

But the "three-month friendship contract" I'd promised her was already bursting its boundaries. Not only was she treating me like more than just a friend, but I was finding it harder to stay just "in like" with her. Yet I was afraid to let her into my heart. "Like" was a street with exits, but "love" was an expressway with no off-ramps. It was better to keep a little distance—for both our sakes.

The following week, Ginny invited me to her apartment for dinner. Back in June she'd promised me a barbequed-rib dinner, and tonight she was going to prepare it.

As I pulled my car up to the curb, she stepped out of her apartment and flashed her million-watt smile. "Do you want me to help you down the hill, or should I call my neighbors?" she asked.

I had forgotten about the five steps leading down to her apartment. For the average person, they would be little more than a hop, skip, and a jump. But to me they were a mountain. Ginny's offer to help me down the grassy sloping hillside was sweet, but naive. I knew it would be impossible for us to control such a descent. As much as I hated to ask for help, I knew we would have to.

"Why don't you call your neighbors, Ginny? It'll be safer for you—and a lot safer for me."

A few moments later two college students came out of the adjacent apartment. They tipped my wheelchair back on its big wheels, with the front casters four feet off the ground, and then bounced me down the steps.

I resented the obstacle those steps presented, knowing all too well how dangerous they could be. Even the strongest guys could slip, and I'd land in a hospital with a broken leg—maybe for a year. My bones didn't heal as well now that I was paralyzed. Was risking a year of my life for a rib dinner a good gamble? And that same mountain would confront us later in the evening when it was time to go home. I'd make sure I left early enough to get help from the young men again before they went to bed. *I won't try this again*, I promised myself.

"Welcome!" Ginny said cheerily as I entered her apartment.

The sweet scent of a vanilla candle burning in the entryway greeted me. And a piano tape played softly in the background. I noticed immediately that the yellow shades and wood tones she used in her decorating were soft and warm, just like her personality.

"This is a beautiful living room set," I said, eyeing the brightly colored flower-print couch and loveseat that graced the left wall.

"My former roommate, Jane, and I took an upholstery class and redid the loveseat ourselves," Ginny said proudly. "But we paid to have the sofa redone because the project was taking up so much of our time."

"Sounds like the two of you bit off a little more than you could chew," I chuckled. Ginny's determination to get things done was admirable. From what I knew of her already, she seemed to be able to do anything she set her mind to.

"I don't think I'll ever tackle a job like that again. And this is my prized Fischer console piano," she said, lifting the keyboard cover. "I bought it at a really great close-out sale a few years ago."

"I know you play the flute—you also play the piano?"

"I started piano in the third grade and flute lessons in the sixth."

Talented girl, I thought.

"But it got to be too much for me to keep up with both," she went on. "So in the ninth grade I dropped piano and continued on with my flute. Now I mainly play the piano for my own enjoyment. Of course, I need it when I'm writing my flute arrangements."

Scanning the room again, I could see that almost everything, including the pictures on the walls and the knick-knacks on the end tables, reflected Ginny's feminine touch.

As we moved toward the kitchen, the smell of baking pastry wafted through the air. I watched Ginny open the oven door and pull out what looked like a pie. But it didn't smell like a dessert. *What in the world is in there?* I wondered.

Ginny caught my questioning glance and explained, "I hope you'll like this beef broccoli pie, Tom. It's a new recipe I just found. I thought it would be fun for us to try it."

What could I say? I hadn't planned on being a guinea pig. Didn't that new best-selling book claim that *Real Men Don't Eat Quiche? Real men might not pay for quiche*, I thought, *but bachelors eat whatever they're served.*

"Sure, Ginny, I'll try it!"

"I know I promised you a barbequed rib dinner," she apologized. "But with working and all, I just didn't have the energy to get it together. The beef-broccoli pie was something I could make ahead and freeze, then pop in the oven today."

"Don't worry about it. The pie smells wonderful. It'll be great!"

I watched as she leaned against the counter to steady herself. Then she put her crutches aside and slid the steaming dish out.

"Ginny, can I help you?" I asked, rolling closer.

"No thanks, I'm doing fine."

"I know how hard it must be for you to cook. I spent a couple of months trying when I was on crutches, but I eventually gave up."

"Do you cook more now that you're in a wheelchair?" Ginny asked, as she poured dressing on the salad.

"More T.V. dinners, maybe, but not real cooking. I used to fix lasagne and chili and spaghetti . . ."

"But you don't anymore?"

"No, it's too dangerous—at least for the benefit you get out of it."

"What do you mean—dangerous?" Ginny asked.

"Two ways. First, eating my cooking is dangerous for others," I chuckled. "And cooking is dangerous for me. Trying to move hot dishes from one place to another on my lap can result in bad spills and burns."

She smiled. "Well, Tom, all you have to do tonight is bless it and eat it."

Minutes later, as we sat at the table eating our tossed salads, I asked Ginny, "How in the world do you bring in your groceries after you go shopping?"

She paused, her fork poised over her salad. "I really don't go shopping that much. When I leave work I'm just too tired to cook. I eat a lot of hearty salads, or I pick up things at drive-thru's."

"Drive-thrus—that's something we have in common."

"But when I do have a lot of grocery bags to bring in, I ask the clerks to pack them light, and I make several trips. Or sometimes my neighbors help. But there was one time when I didn't know what to do. It was about two o'clock in the afternoon, and no one was around. I was preparing for company and had about six heavy bags to bring in."

"What did you do?" I asked.

"Well, I sat in my car for about fifteen minutes, thinking surely someone would come along, but no one did. So I prayed that God would send an angel to help me."

"And what happened?"

"You won't believe it, Tom, but this is what really happened. As I opened the trunk to lift out the groceries, a car pulled up behind me and a friendly voice called out, 'Hey, Miss, you need some help?' When I looked around to see who it was, I could hardly believe my eyes."

"Was it an angel?" I asked.

She chuckled. "Well, he didn't have flowing white robes. But he was one of the check-out boys from the grocery store where I'd been shopping. He had finished work and 'just happened' to be driving by, so he offered to carry all my bags in for me. Isn't that incredible?"

I gazed at her. It wasn't hard to imagine that God had sent a check-out boy just for Ginny in her time of need. *It must be great to have that kind of faith*, I thought.

Ginny gingerly moved the beef-broccoli pie from the serving cart to the table, then sliced a huge piece for me and a smaller one for herself. *I hope I like it*, I thought.

"Is it O.K., Tom?" she asked as I sampled my third bite.

I hesitated. "It's tasty—though I must admit I've never had anything quite like it before. The best part about it,

Ginny," I added brightly, "is that you cared enough to fix it for me."

"Thanks," she said, beaming back at me. "But I'm still planning to fix you that rib dinner sometime. I'll give you a rain check, O.K.?"

"Sounds great," was my first response. But then I thought, *How can I tell this sweet girl that the steps in front of her apartment are just too much of a hassle?* I didn't want to risk being carried down them again.

Changing the subject, I asked, "Don't you play your flute this Saturday in your friends' wedding?"

"You sure have a good memory!"

"I've been hoping that maybe you'd invite me to come along. I'd love to hear you play."

Her eyes lit up. "Really? I'd love to have you come! I wanted to invite you, but I was afraid to."

"Afraid? What could you be afraid of?" In fact, I had actually been feeling hurt because she hadn't asked me. *Was she reluctant to be seen dating a handicapped person?* I wondered.

"I was afraid you'd think it very forward of me—inviting you to a wedding. I was afraid I'd scare you away. I had no idea that you might want to come. It would be great to have you there."

I was up and ready early on Saturday morning. We had agreed to meet at my condo, then drive over to church together. As I sat waiting for her and gazing out at the sun dancing on the pool, I wondered what the day would hold. Ginny was becoming harder to resist. Her winsome ways, pixie eyes, and sweet disposition were disarming me. I had to slow down my thoughts of her.

Can I risk loving a handicapped girl? I wondered. Will people think I can't do any better? And who are the "theys" I'm always so concerned about anyway? Is it my own insecurities, and not Ginny's handicap, that make me always worry about what people might be thinking?

Suddenly, I was jarred from my thoughts by Ginny's familiar voice calling out from my open front doorway. "Good morning, Tom. Wow!" she said, eyeing my suit. "Gray is a great color for you."

"I have to look my best—my date is one of the stars of the show, you know. You look pretty terrific yourself," I said, reaching up to give her a hug. She looked beautiful in her apricot-colored, floor-length gown.

"We better get going so you have time to get your flute warmed up," I warned her.

The wedding was to be held in the chapel behind the Free Church sanctuary. It could seat about 400 people, more than the average church, but it was still small compared to the 2500-seat sanctuary in the front. The inside walls were bare gray stone; the only color came from the plants, flowers, and candelabras brought in especially for the wedding ceremony.

"These are two of my best friends—Elaine and Bernie Minton," Ginny said, as we entered the chapel. They greeted her with a hug and a kiss and shook hands with me. I'd never met any of Ginny's friends before. I wondered if they were thinking, *Can't she do any better than a guy in a wheelchair?* This was Ginny's church and the tables were turned. Now I, not Ginny, was the unknown on display.

Elaine smiled at me. "Ginny tells me you work for Bechtel. Bernie works right down the street at Powerine. You guys will have a lot in common to talk about. Why don't you sit with us?"

Before I could reply, Ginny interrupted, "Tom, that will be great for you. I have to sit on the platform throughout the whole wedding. In fact, I need to go up front right now for a sound check. I'll talk to you later."

During the next fifteen minutes I learned a little bit about the Mintons and a lot about how wonderful they thought Ginny was. I also learned that Elaine and Ginny had been prayer partners for years.

A warm glow filled the room as the ushers lit the candles. Then Ginny's clear a cappella flute, playing "Morning Has Broken," lilted through the silence. It sent shivers along my spine. It had been the weekly call to worship at GGCC a few years back when I was, so to speak, "cutting my teeth on Christianity." This song had always touched me deeply, but there was something extra special in hearing Ginny play it.

After the ceremony and closing prayer, Ginny played "My Tribute." As I closed my eyes to listen, it seemed as if God's Holy Spirit was permeating all my being.

I thought of the last time I'd heard that song. My friend, Becky, who had been completely healed of Multiple Sclerosis, had stood there singing, "How can I say thanks for the things You have done for me," at her brother's wedding. I hoped and prayed that someday soon that same physical healing would come to me as well.

Tears welled in my eyes as my thoughts shifted from Becky back to the courageous young woman on the platform. Then suddenly my tears became a flood, and I began to shake uncontrollably. I had never lost control of my emotions like this before. Crying at weddings was acceptable behavior—even for men—at times. But I was crying at the wedding of two total strangers.

"Tom, are you all right?" Elaine whispered, reaching over with a handkerchief. She looked puzzled.

"It's a long story, Elaine," I whispered back between my sobs.

11

Please Love Me

Ginny

It was Monday morning. The events of the past month swirled through my mind as I sat drinking my morning coffee and gazing out the window.

So Tom and I have a three-month friendship contract, I thought. How could he reduce our relationship to "contract" level—as if it were one of his Bechtel jobs with an evaluation and a project completion date? *Can I survive this craziness?* I asked myself.

I sensed that this must be Tom's escape route if things didn't work out between us. But I was willing to take the gamble. Maybe God does have something in mind for us, and maybe Tom will fall in love with me someday. What have I got to lose?

As friends we'd have the opportunity to get to know each other better, to see if our hangups and differences could be resolved. Tom was the first guy I'd ever really cared for who also wanted to date and spend time with me on a regular basis. I loved his great sense of humor, and he seemed to enjoy my company, too. But he had so many walls built up around himself. Why? What was he afraid of?

Did his childhood and the instability of his home life have something to do with it? By the time he was in the seventh grade, he'd lost all three of his moms—first his natural mother, then his Aunt Hazel, and then his sister Jane when she got married. After that, he was pretty much on his own. *Maybe he doesn't even know what real love is—and that it can last.*

I picked up the book lying on the table, *Please Love Me* by Keith Miller. It too was about someone who had experienced a lot of insecurities as a child and was searching for the miracle of a meaningful friendship and love. What was Tom trying to tell me by asking me to read this book? Was he searching for love just as much as I was?

I remembered how he had wept uncontrollably at the wedding on Saturday when I played *My Tribute*. It comforted me to know that maybe Tom didn't have his life totally together either, as I'd originally thought. Maybe he had some insecurities, too.

Since it was my day off, I decided to finish reading *Please Love Me*. By the time I'd reached the end of the book, I was sobbing. I was deeply moved by the young woman in the story who didn't know whether she would still be accepted if she revealed her true self.

Will Tom ever love me if I really open myself up to him? I wondered. *What would he think if he knew how tired I get and how hard it is for me to do even simple tasks at times?* I didn't know; only God knew. I'd have to trust him for the answers.

As much as I wanted to think of Tom only as a friend, I couldn't. The more I tried to suppress my feelings, the stronger they grew. There was no getting around it. I was deeply in love with him and I wanted his love in return. The tears came again.

When I thought about his "contract" offer, feelings of hurt and irritation ran through my veins. Then when I remembered his considerate nature and how he'd surprised me with a special dinner the other night, feelings of love flooded through me. I felt so confused.

Certainly Tom had expanded my world beyond what I'd ever known before. He was very much the successful businessman I had dreamed of marrying. Yet in many other ways, he was very down-to-earth. Whether it was an elegant dinner or a hamburger, we had fun together. In spite of some of his crazy ideas—like the "contract" deal—Tom was my kind of guy.

Suddenly, a telephone ring pierced the silence of my empty apartment. It rang again. I lifted the receiver.

"Hello," I whispered as I wiped the salty dampness from my cheeks.

"Ginny, are you okay?" Tom's familiar voice came over the line. "It sounds like you've been crying."

"I'm fine. I just finished reading *Please Love Me*," I said, not wanting to reveal the real reason for my tears. I was ecstatic to hear his voice. I'd wanted so much to talk with him, but I knew I couldn't call.

"It *is* a moving story. Now that we've both read it, we'll have to discuss it sometime."

"Yes, let's do—soon," I responded eagerly.

"Okay, but for now, I've got a question for you. I've been asked to be the North Orange County publicity chairman for the new 'Joni' film. It's going to be released soon."

"Oh, I'm glad. With your background in public relations, you'll be great for the job."

"I hope so. But I need a co-chair to help me. How would you like the job, Ginny?"

Would I like the job? I could hardly believe my ears. "I'd love to help you," I answered, trying not to sound too excited. "When do we get started?"

"Tomorrow night. There's a meeting with a representative of Worldwide Pictures and some of the other workers in the area. I'd like you to come with me."

"Just tell me when to be ready."

"I'll pick you up right after work. We'll grab a bite to eat and then go on over to the meeting. Can you be ready at five o'clock?"

"I'll be ready."

"See you then. And Ginny—God loves you, and so do I."

I was thrilled to think I'd be seeing Tom on a regular basis, at least until the film was released. Maybe God would use our work to bring us closer together.

But glad as I was, I knew there was one thing we needed to get resolved. Even though Tom was handicapped himself, I could tell he was uptight about mine. He had never mentioned that my disability bothered him, but I sensed that it did. I knew that he'd dated a lot of beautiful girls in the past. Maybe it was hard for him to be seen with a girl who walked with a leg brace and two crutches.

What would happen if I confronted him? Would he become more distant? I'd have to risk it. *If he can't accept me the way I am, then maybe this friendship isn't worth pursuing.*

Following Tuesday night's meeting, Tom and I decided to meet again on Saturday to discuss the publicity plans. So after an early dinner, we went to Tom's condo to write out some of our goals.

"Before we get started, Ginny, why don't we go outside for awhile and enjoy the warm summer evening," Tom suggested.

As we moved out onto the patio, I gazed up at the puffy pink clouds, highlighted by rosy hues of the setting sun. For a moment I stood in awe, soaking in the beauty displayed in the skies. *The heavens truly do declare the glory of God*, I marveled.

Tom's place sure is beautiful, I thought, as I sat down on a large rock near the stream running behind his unit. The waterfalls, towering pines, and lush foliage made it seem like a mountain resort in the midst of the city.

"Tom, does it bother you," I said shyly, "to be seen with a handicapped girl?"

Tom's relaxed expression suddenly grew tense. He seemed to be miles away.

"Be honest with me. I want to know," I pressed.

"Why do you ask that, Ginny?" he said, turning toward me.

"Sometimes you seem to be so uptight about being with me. And whenever we pray together you always ask God to heal me."

"I guess it's a lot more obvious than I thought," he apologized.

My pulse raced, and my face grew warm. I knew I had limitations, but didn't everybody? I'd never really considered myself *handicapped*.

How can you feel that way? I chided him silently. *You're handicapped, too. Who do you think you are, anyway?*

However, as I sat there staring straight ahead, I realized that I, too, had been looking for the perfect man. Before Tom, I would never have believed I'd fall in love with someone in a wheelchair. But when I met Tom, I found in him everything I'd ever hoped for.

"Maybe it's my own insecurities that make me uncomfortable about dating you," he went on. "Certainly, Ginny, you're the most wonderful person I've ever known. You always seem to look into people's hearts and see the beauty God has placed there. All my life I've been so concerned with the external, with physical appearances."

He looked discouraged and confused, as if he thought he'd never be able to change his way of thinking.

A tear slipped down my cheek as I gazed up into the sky. I was discouraged, too. I watched my weight carefully and did everything I could to keep myself as physically attractive as possible. Yet, there was nothing I could do about my leg brace and crutches. How I wanted Tom to see *beyond* my handicap and *into my heart!*

I'd always hoped that when the right guy came along my handicap would not be a big roadblock in our relationship. But would Tom be able to accept me as I was? Or would it be my disability that would keep him from falling in love with me?

A light breeze rustled through the trees behind us and the scent of flowering jasmine lingered in the air. But a wrenching pain lingered in my heart. I had thought our handicaps might bond us together. Now I wondered if it would be just the opposite.

"Ginny, I wish I could see other people through God's eyes—like you do," Tom's wistful voice broke the silence.

"You can, Tom," I encouraged him. "You will. I know you will." I groped for the right words. "None of us, in and of ourselves, has the ability to see others through God's eyes. That can only happen with the help of God's Spirit. He's had a lot of time to work on me and to make me more like him. You've only been a committed Christian for two years. It takes time."

He looked at me affectionately. "Your loving spirit, Ginny, has taught me so much about God and his love already. Pray that God will help me to be more like him, too."

I nodded. "I will, Tom, I promise I will."

Maneuvering his chair closer to me, he reached up and tenderly brushed a tear from my cheek. Then taking my hand in his, he leaned over and placed a gentle kiss on my lips. "Ginny," he whispered, "God is already beginning to open my eyes more than I'd ever dreamed possible."

12

Who's Handicapped, Anyway?

—

Tom

"You've got a surprise coming," I told Ginny as we drove down Harbor Boulevard in my convertible, the palm trees swaying gently above us. It was a warm August Saturday evening, and she looked tanned and beautiful in her sleeveless white dress.

"I do?" she said, smiling with delight. "Where are we going?" She was so unpretentious and easy to be with. Surprising her was going to be fun.

"If I told you, then it wouldn't be a surprise."

"Give me a hint," she cajoled.

"No! I'm going to keep you guessing for awhile. I know how you love surprises," I teased, pulling the car into a shopping plaza and up to the curb. "The first stop is right here. Skinny Haven for a really healthy, low-fat, low-sugar, and low-calorie dinner. I hope you'll like it."

"Oh, that sounds great. I'm always trying to watch my weight."

"Me too. It seems like once you gain a few pounds, they're harder to lose than bill collectors. Why don't you get out here, Ginny, and I'll park the car. Then you won't have to walk so far."

"I'll go put our name in," she agreed as she slipped out of her seat and stepped easily up the curb. For me, curbs were a major problem; for Ginny, it was distance. I was glad I could chauffeur her to the door almost everywhere we went.

How did she ever manage in Hong Kong? I wondered, remembering her short-term mission to the Far East. *Who chauffeured her there? And what challenges did she face living in a totally different part of the world?* Finding out more about her adventures in the Orient would make for interesting dinner conversation.

After being seated, I asked her, "Weren't you afraid when you went to Hong Kong? Of going halfway around the world all by yourself?"

"I wasn't really by myself," she said, reaching for her glass of water. "Karen, a nurse friend from my church in St. Paul, went too. Her cousin Bonnie is married to Dr. Gordon Addington, who was the hospital medical superintendent at that time. So Karen wrote and inquired about the possibility of helping out at the hospital.

"I'd known for several months that they needed a medical technologist, but I couldn't imagine it being me, and I couldn't imagine going alone. But when Karen said she was going, I said, 'Count me in.' "

I grinned. "God really worked that one out, didn't he?"

"He really did. Karen was a wonderful roommate and friend. We had a lot of fun exploring Hong Kong together in our free time. Without her help, I never could have focused my energy on setting up the lab like I did. Although we paid a little Chinese lady to clean for us every week, Karen did all the shopping and most of the cooking, too."

"Did you have a car over there?" I asked, as the waitress placed our chicken dinners on the table.

"Hong Kong is so crowded that not many people do. But we didn't really need one, anyway. The apartment the hospital rented for us was only a short half-block walk. And I became good friends with one of the lab techs we hired. Irene was a native of Hong Kong and had a car, and we did a lot of things together. And Karen dated a Baptist missionary who took the two of us around. There were taxis, too. We'd just go out in the street and hail one down."

"What about curb cuts?"

"I saw very few. You would have had a tough time."

"So you probably didn't see many people in wheelchairs."

"A lot of the older folks there use fancy carved wooden canes. But I hardly ever saw anyone in a wheelchair," Ginny said, sipping her coffee. "I guess handicapped people just don't get out like we do here in the States. In fact, wherever I went in Hong Kong, people would just stop and stare at me, as if I were from outer space or something. It made me feel awkward at first, but I got used to it. What else could I do? I'd just smile and keep going. In fact, it was during those first few weeks in Hong Kong I made the decision not to let that kind of thing bother me. If I were to worry," she continued, "about what each and every person thought of me and how I looked, I'd waste my entire life and never accomplish anything."

I nodded. The more time I spent with Ginny, the more I began to realize that being handicapped sometimes has a lot more to do with a person's attitude than physical condition. "You're right. Worrying about things you'll never be able to change is counter-productive. I know of people who rarely get out of the house because they're afraid to be seen in a wheelchair—and end up missing a lot of what life has to offer."

"I've heard some stories like that too," Ginny said, shaking her head. "My philosophy is, *Use whatever you've got to use and do whatever you've got to do to get on with your life.*"

I admired Ginny's determination and acceptance of her situation. I wondered if I would have been as well-adjusted as she—a twenty-three-year-old in a strange country—had been.

"What about the heat over there? I've heard that Hong Kong is really hot and humid. Didn't that bother you?"

"It would have been terrible; the humidity was in the 90's almost all the time. But Dr. Addington anticipated that problem and made arrangements to have an air conditioner installed in the lab before I arrived. So, even though our apartment wasn't air-conditioned, it was cool in the lab where I spent most of my time."

"How were you ever able to afford that trip, Ginny? Money was my biggest concern my first year out of college."

"It wasn't really that expensive, Tom. Besides the apartment, the hospital also provided us with a small monthly salary. All we had to pay for was the round trip plane fare—$1100. Most of the money came from my home church in Winona and from the church I was attending in St. Paul, Minnesota. And family and friends gave a little bit more. I never asked anybody for a dime, but my younger brother, Dave, and his youth group did. They did odd jobs, held a car wash, even set up a 'dime-a-dish for Ginny' buffet dinner to help raise money for my trip. What a blessing they were."

As Ginny went on with her story, I fought an urge to put my arms around her and cry. *What an incredible woman*, I thought. In spite of her handicap, she gave a year and a half of her life for a missionary venture. And it was obvious that in addition to the service she had given, she'd also been richly blessed. I was awed by her courage—traveling to another country, learning a new language, and setting up an entire medical laboratory.

Suddenly it was time to go. Though I was reluctant to cut short her fascinating story of faith in action, I knew there would be other chances as the summer went on. After all, her "three-month contract" still had seven weeks to go.

"I'm going to use the restroom here," I told her, finishing up my last bite of baked potato. "There may not be a wheelchair accessible one where we're going."

As I started toward the restroom, the crowded tables and chairs cut me off from a direct line to the back. Three sets of diners rose and pulled their chairs in to let me pass. When I finally go there, I stared at the door. It was a small one, probably less than twenty-four inches wide. Even my narrow wheelchair was too wide to get through.

"No go," I announced, returning to Ginny, who sat sipping her last few drops of coffee. "I'll have to try the bathroom at the church."

"Church?" she said with a puzzled look. "Are we going to church?"

"We'd better get moving," I said, smiling as I tried to cover my slip-up. "You know how long it takes to get in the car."

"Where is the car?" Ginny asked.

"Over there," I said, pointing to the right, as we left the restaurant. "But you wait here and I'll go get it."

I rolled down the curb cut and whizzed past her as she stood waiting patiently on the sidewalk. Reaching the car, I quickly opened the door and threw my leg-rests off, then prepared to slide into the driver's seat. My watch showed we only had half an hour. How would we ever make it on time?

As I started to swing my body into the car, the passenger door suddenly opened, and Ginny stepped in.

"Hey, what are you doing?" I scolded. "I didn't want you to have to walk this far."

"I know you're in a hurry, Tom, and I don't want to make us late. It wasn't that far," she said cheerily.

I stared at her in amazement. It was true she couldn't walk as far or as fast as I could roll. But walking enabled her to take shortcuts, like stepping down a curb or going through a narrow door, that all my speed couldn't match. And her patience, not pretending she could or had to do everything at a breakneck speed, was so unlike me. Whereas I'd get upset about things like a person illegally parking in a handicapped space, she was able to ignore the situation. I was beginning to see that physically and emotionally I was more handicapped than she was.

Only fifteen minutes later, we pulled into a church parking lot. "Oh, Tom," Ginny exclaimed, her face lighting up. "That sign says Kelly Willard is here tonight. This is a wonderful surprise."

"She's my favorite singer. I hope you'll like her as much as I do. After all, you're the musician," I said, as we entered the church. "I'm going to check out the men's room. Pick an aisle seat and save me a parking space, okay?" I winked at her as I rolled away.

Six minutes later I was back.

"How was it?" Ginny asked.

"Good—they've widened the doors."

"I'm glad," she sighed with a look of relief.

"Sometimes you must wonder about the dumb things I get uptight about."

"Well, I certainly can't blame you for being upset about inaccessible restrooms. I would be too. But sometimes you do tend to overanalyze things."

"Maybe it's being an engineer. I'm always looking for perfection."

The audience grew quiet. "I think," Ginny whispered, "We each need to make the best of our circumstances, whatever they are. My dad used to tell us kids, 'Just do your best.' That was good advice."

I looked into her eyes. Ginny wasn't advocating mediocrity; she was a realist. She served her church, her employer, her friends, giving her best and not being afraid to admit her limitations. I'd never been willing to accept mine. It was important that I prove to others I could still do the same things I did before MS crippled my body. Maybe Ginny had an advantage in being handicapped early in life. She wasn't carrying around a load of old—and now unrealistic—expectations and dreams.

A few minutes later the concert began with Kelly Willard sitting at the piano singing a lively praise song, "Let's Forget About Ourselves." After the first several verses, she invited the audience to clap and sing along with her. I started to clap my hands, but as I saw Ginny sitting there grinning at me, I took her hand instead. It was soft and warm and so responsive. I felt a joy in being with her that I'd never known before.

As we sat there hand in hand, singing the words, "Let's forget about ourselves and magnify the Lord and worship him," it finally dawned on me why Ginny wasn't self-conscious or uptight about my handicap—or her own. It was, as the song said, because her eyes were on the Lord—and not on her earthly circumstances. She had learned to deal with her problems, but she didn't dwell on them.

As we continued to sing, I squeezed her hand and prayed silently, *Help me, Lord, to forget about myself . . . to magnify you . . . and worship you.*

13

God Loves You, and So Do I

Ginny

As I sat at the kitchen table writing my parents a long overdue letter, the sound of the telephone jarred me from my thoughts. My hand trembled as I picked up the receiver. Could it be Tom? He'd promised to call me from Portland sometime this week.

"Hi, beautiful!" Tom's enthusiastic voice echoed. "How's the world's greatest woman tonight?"

"I'm doing great, but I miss you," I said, my heart pounding. "How is the conference going?"

"Super! Portland's beautiful, the air is crystal clear, and the food's a bachelor's heaven. You wouldn't believe the buffet they had for us last night. All the ham and prime-rib sandwiches, fresh shrimp cocktails, oysters Rockefeller, cavier . . ."

"Wait a minute. I thought you went there to speak, not eat."

"Well, I'm doing a little of both. You know me—I never pass up a free meal."

I laughed. "Sounds like your health food diet really went out the window last night. How did your speech go—the one you were doing for the chemical engineers?"

"It went great, too. Thirty people came to my seminar. A couple of them were company vice-presidents, and they really got excited about setting up public information programs like we've done at Bechtel," he said proudly.

Tom was obviously on an emotional high. I loved having him share his successes with me, and I was so happy for him. But at the same time, I was afraid that the more involved he got with his career, the less time he'd have for me.

"It sounds like you did a great job," I said, trying to hide my mixed emotions.

"But that's not why I called you, Ginny," he went on. "I wanted to tell you about a movie I watched on cable T.V. in my room earlier tonight. It was about a guy who was looking for the perfect woman."

"And how was it?" I asked nonchalantly, wondering how two hours of looking at the perfect woman would affect him. Certainly I knew I'd never be perfect—at least, not physically.

"Very revealing, Ginny. I used to think that physical beauty was a woman's most important quality. But, as this movie so clearly illustrated, great beauty can be very shallow. I'm glad you're not only beautiful on the outside, Ginny," he said softly, "but on the inside, too."

I was touched and surprised. "I'll give you a rain check on a big hug and kiss for that one, Tom."

"A-l-l-r-i-g-h-t!" he exclaimed.

By the time we finally said our good-byes, I was flying high, too. *Maybe Tom is getting over some of his hangups about us*, I mused. Ever since he'd taken me to the Kelly Willard concert, he'd been different. He seemed warmer, friendlier, more comfortable with me. I was enjoying every minute of it.

Later that week, Tom and I attended another wedding. We held hands as Tom's friends exchanged their vows under a backyard gazebo. With the setting sun adding an extra touch of romance to the evening, I sat there wondering, *Will Tom and I ever share a time like this?*

The next weekend we went to yet another wedding, the third that month. The wedding was a big, elaborate one. As the groom, in his white tuxedo, walked his new bride, in her exquisite, long white gown, back up the aisle, my heart skipped a beat. Would I ever see the day when I would walk down the aisle to meet Tom?

After a fancy reception at a hilltop estate, we drove down to the ocean to enjoy the rest of the evening.

"Since we're in the area, I'll show you my old beachfront home," Tom said, pulling into a condominium complex.

"It must have been great, living so close to the ocean."

"Actually it was frustrating. The beach was right across the road, but it was a world away for me because my legs were too weak to walk to it. And my unit really wasn't set up for a wheelchair anyway."

"Couldn't you have modified it to fit your needs?"

"When I bought it, I still believed I would beat MS. It wasn't until a year later that I found out I wouldn't. By then I knew I had to find a place with a swimming pool."

Tom stared straight ahead at his old building. "I got so depressed about my MS," he continued. "At work I was using a wheelchair I'd borrowed from the MS Society. But

when I got home at night, I'd practically have to crawl from
my car to the condo. I kept thinking I'd get better, but I never
did."

Tears of compassion filled my eyes as I listened. "Oh,
Tom, if I'd only known you back then, I'd have tried to
help . . ."

"You're so sweet, Ginny," Tom said, shaking his head,
"but I doubt if you'd have liked me in those days. I wasn't
living like a Christian, that's for sure . . . But, to get on with
my story, one of my bachelor buddies from work came and
lived with me. I needed a roommate, and he needed a place
to stay. He was a great friend to me during that time in my
life."

"Then what?"

"I went to Rancho Los Amigos Hospital. There a wonderful physical therapist convinced me I could lead a fuller and
more productive life from a wheelchair. It would be better
than trying to hobble and crawl around with canes and
crutches."

"It sure sounds like you made the right move."

"But it was so hard at first. I must have cried for hours
after my therapist told me she was not going to teach me to
walk again but how to be functional in a wheelchair. I hated
the thought that people might think less of me because I was
now in a wheelchair."

I reached over and placed my hand on his. "Tom, from the
day I met you, I've always thought you were the greatest.
Look how well you've done since you got your chair. It's
hardly slowed you down at all."

"I am thankful now. In fact, it was this wheelchair that
slowed me down enough for God to get my attention."

"Then it's been a blessing in disguise, right?"

Tom smiled. "You can say that again. I'd much rather be rolling in this wheelchair with the Lord than walking without him."

I squeezed his hand.

"Why don't we go down to Huntington Beach?" Tom suggested. "The city just put in a paved wheelchair path across the sand."

It was a short drive, and within minutes we were out of the car and heading toward the ocean on the paved walkway. A light breeze carried the fresh ocean air into our nostrils. Waves lapped against the sand, and a swooping seagull searched for its dinner.

Tom watched as an oil tanker slowly edged its way along the horizon. But my gaze wandered off to the west, where a fiery reddish-orange sunset began to explode on the horizon.

Today had been an almost perfect day. Tom had stayed near me at the reception and seemed to be proud I was his date. And now we were back at the ocean again—the same ocean, although a different beach—where this crazy "love-like" friendship had begun three months ago.

"You must be getting tired," he said, motioning for me to sit on his lap.

He didn't need to ask me twice.

"Tom, this has been such a wonderful day. Thank you," I said softly. "I love you, and I love being with you."

He was momentarily speechless, obviously surprised by my remark. Then, looking directly into my eyes, he replied, "I know you do, Ginny. But you're too good for me."

His words pierced my heart like a knife. The belief that God had spared my life so I could do something great for him had propelled me to excellence in academics, music, and in almost everything I tried. But now I felt as if life had lost its sparkle. I could do anything but win Tom's heart.

Suddenly, the pain of rejection overwhelmed me, and I began to cry. I couldn't hold back the tears any longer.

"Ginny," Tom said, as he caressed my arm, "there's so much bad stuff in my past. I've only been a committed Christian for two years. I've got such a long way to go."

I felt like I was on an emotional rollercoaster, riding from joy to frustration, to despair, and now back to feelings of compassion and love.

"Tom, I love you . . . just the way you are. I'm not looking for a super-Christian or a perfect man. And I'm not too good for you," I blurted out between my sobs. "But if you still think I am, then tell me what I can do to be worse."

Tom seemed stunned for a moment. Then his strained expression turned into a grin. "So, you agree you're too good for me, eh? Only you could get away with saying that. I want you to stay the sweet and beautiful person you are. And I'm going to pray that God will make me into the man he wants me to be."

"I think you're already wonderful," I said. "The Bible says that when you accept Christ into your life, you become an entirely new person inside. God forgets about your old sinful ways and gives you a chance to begin again."

Putting his arm around my shoulder, he drew me close. His arms encircling me made me feel warm and secure. *Please, let us stay here like this forever,* I silently pleaded with God.

"Tom, I really do love you," I repeated, leaning back against his chest.

Giving me a little squeeze, he whispered his usual response, "Ginny, God loves you, and so do I."

His words stung me. *I know God loves me, but will you ever love me? He can say the "God loves you" cliché to anyone and still feel safe*, I thought, in total frustration.

Tom was hard to read. At times he was so tender and warm, but then he'd put up all his defenses—keeping me at a safe distance from his emotions. How many more unpredictable ups and downs could I endure?

As a rush of total discouragement flooded over me, I blurted out, "Tom, if you don't love me, will you please pray that God will send a wonderful Christian man into my life who will?" I didn't even care what he thought of such a request. I was so tired of pretending and playing games.

He looked at me quizzically, his eyes twinkling. Then in his typical boyish way, he quipped, "Did you have any specific names in mind?"

14

A
Once-in-a-Lifetime
Chance?

Tom

This is where it all began, I thought, as I sat in the Free Church sanctuary with Ginny. On a warm holiday Sunday evening just like this, barely three months ago, I had reached out to help a "sad-faced little crippled girl." Now she was radiant and beautiful as we were introduced to the congregation as co-chairs of publicity for the new "Joni" movie.

After the service, several people came up to talk with Ginny about the film. It was obvious how much they loved her. Everyone seemed to love Ginny. Even Bob and Randi, at their wedding yesterday, had pulled me aside to tell me how special they thought she was. Why was I struggling so with my feelings for her?

I still couldn't figure out if I was in "like"—or in love with her. Ginny certainly made me feel more loved than I'd ever felt before. And I'd certainly felt more of God's love reaching out to me in the past three months than ever before, too. But was love enough?

My heart pulled me in one direction, but my brain kept echoing all the reasons why it wouldn't work—why it *couldn't* work. We were from two different worlds. Ginny lived in a peaceful, beautiful, family-centered world, whereas mine was a competitive, driving, lonely world. She'd accepted Jesus into her life when she was only four and a half years old. I'd been a committed Christian for only the past two years. My mind kept analyzing, trying to figure things out.

"We'd better get moving or we'll be the last ones to leave again," I said, as Ginny finished speaking with a friend. But before she could respond, an older man—wearing a short-sleeved shirt and tie, and carrying a Bible—approached. His strong, decisive stride exuded confidence.

"Ginny, I haven't seen you in awhile. What have you been up to?" the man said, with a twinkle in his eye and a broad, knowing smile.

"Hi, Neil. This is my friend Tom," Ginny grinned back at him. "We've been working on the film together."

"Glad to meet you, Tom. I'm Neil Logsdon," he declared, looking at me with a warm glance of acceptance. "Why don't you two join us for toasted cheese sandwiches at our house tonight? I know Cora would love to meet your friend, too."

"Well, how about it, Tom?" Ginny asked.

"Great! You know how I love home-cooked meals!"

As we left the church, I commented, "These people must be special friends of yours. Most folks don't just invite you over on the spur of the moment like this—especially not in California."

"They *are* special," Ginny explained. "I first heard about them in Hong Kong through their daughter and son-in-law,

Betty and George Simms. George was a doctor at our hospital when I was there."

"Ah-ha," I teased her, "I'll bet they really gave Neil and Cora the inside scoop on you."

Ginny laughed as she admitted, "When I finally met the Logsdons here at the church, they did seem to know a lot about me. Then we became good friends when we served on the deacon board together." Ginny was so much fun to kid. I knew the reports from Hong Kong must have brimmed with praise for this exceptional young lady.

"Toasted cheese sandwiches bring back memories of my high school days," I said, as we drove along the tree-lined street past older single-story homes. "They were a mainstay of my cooking menu, along with hamburgers and hot dogs, when I was chef for my dad and me. He was a gas station attendant, so we couldn't afford meat very often. Sometimes cheese sandwiches were the best we could do."

"I know what you mean. We ate them a lot, too," Ginny said, as we arrived at the Logsdons' house.

When I entered the hallway, a sweet-looking lady walked up to me, wiping her hands on a flowered apron.

"Hi, Tom. I'm Neil's wife, Cora," she said warmly as she shook my hand. "We're happy you could come. Everything's just about ready." As the aroma of freshly baked cookies wafted through the air, I sighed. *There goes my diet again.*

The toasted cheese sandwiches were served in a small dining area on paper plates. I was also given my first exposure to real Scandanavian food—savoring an authentic Swedish smorgasbord with many of the goodies Ginny had claimed Swedes were famous for.

During supper Neil and Cora, like proud grandparents, told me what a wonderful girl Ginny was. They bragged about what a great job she'd done setting up the medical lab in Hong Kong and how beautifully she played her flute. If the invitation hadn't been such a spur-of-the-moment thing, I might have suspected that the whole evening was a set-up. But their sweetness and sincerity—just like Ginny's—was real.

"This is really great, Cora," I said, as I scraped the last bit of lime green jello salad off my plate and reached for a lemon square.

"Cora's not only the best cook this side of heaven," Neil boasted with a broad grin, "but the best egg artist, too. She decorates eggshells so they tell a story." Neil walked to a cabinet and pulled out an object the size of a large grapefruit. "This is an ostrich egg. It opens into six parts, chronicling the story of Jesus' life."

I looked closely at the egg. The outer shell was ornately decorated with gold and silver braid and various kinds of jewels, and the inside showcased six three-dimensional scenes. They were works of art.

Neil went to another cabinet. "The eggs in here are too small for me to pick up. Cora would shoot me if I dropped one," he teased.

"Oh, Neil," Cora sighed from the other side of the room, with a look of feigned exasperation. "You know you can take one out for Tom to look at."

"That's okay, Cora. I don't want to get too close," I admitted. "I'm kinda clumsy. I can see through the cabinet that they're beautiful."

"Why don't you go into the bedroom and see Neil's train set and waterbed?" Cora suggested. "I'm sure you'll find that more interesting."

Waterbed, I thought, rolling into the bedroom behind Neil. *For swinging singles maybe, but for senior citizens?*

Neil bounced onto the waterbed and explained. "I injured my back a few years ago, and sleeping on this waterbed helps me a lot. Cora doesn't mind." *How wonderful! I thought,* squooshing my hand on the bed. *Two elderly people still sleeping together, and on a waterbed, no less!* The spirit of their home seemed to represent what God meant when he wrote, "It is not good for man to be alone; I will make him a helper . . . and the two became one."

"And here's my train set," Neil announced, pointing to the maze of tracks mounted on a huge board on one side of the bed. *What's a retired man doing with all this? In his bedroom, no less! Cora must be a mighty loving—and tolerant—woman,* I thought.

"I've got twelve separate trains with a complete twelve-track switching center," Neil reported. Then, with the flip of a switch, one of the trains started onto the main line. It ran past miniature mountain ranges, a river, and a city, finally stopping at a solitary little chapel nestled in a small valley. Within seconds the strains of the hymn, "All Hail the Power of Jesus' Name," drifted up from the chapel. This *was* an unusual bedroom. *These people,* I said to myself, *are somethin' else!*

"Neil, what are these?" I asked, pointing to a shelf filled with cassette tapes.

"Those hold every message ever delivered by Pastor Chuck at the Fullerton Free Church. When that young Swindoll first came here, we sensed his messages were worth keeping and sending to our Free Church missionaries. So we helped start a tape ministry. As you get older, Tom, you learn to recognize value," he said, looking me straight in the eye. "But, if you overlook it, you may never have a second chance."

"What do you mean by that?" I queried.

"Well, you couldn't record those early messages now. Or, take Cora and myself. We had some problems early on in our marriage, before I became a Christian. But we recognized that what we *had* was far more valuable than what we lacked. And we've had forty-six wonderful years together."

When we left their home that evening, I watched Ginny at the doorway as she gave the Logsdons their good-bye hugs. *Where will I be at sixty-five?* I wondered. Probably a confirmed bachelor rolling along in my wheelchair, eating at drive-thru restaurants, and going to ballgames with the guys.

Waiting for the perfect woman, even though I was far from the perfect man, seemed a bleak prospect. But it was still better than a mediocre or bad marriage—two people together in the same house but living separate lives. I'd dated divorcées who told horror stories about the pitfalls of marriage. In fact, the almanac even showed that for every two new marriages there was one divorce. Statistically speaking, the odds for a happy marriage were not good.

But, admittedly, I had just been presented with another alternative: two Spirit-filled people living together as one, just as the Bible said it should be. I had a profound sense that Neil and Cora were two people for whom marriage worked. They each did their own thing and yet they did those things together, complementing one another's strengths and filling in for each other's weaknesses. Cora had been by Neil's side, sharing and developing not only what had become a worldwide tape ministry, but also a beautiful marriage. They had reached the golden years with shared experiences that proved their marriage worked.

As I thought about Neil's comment—"You may never have a second chance"—I began to wonder, *Could it be that Ginny's love is a once-in-a-lifetime chance? Perhaps I should offer to extend her "friendship contract" through Christmas!*

15

Fears for the Future

Ginny

I*t's been such a great summer,* I thought wistfully, as we sat in the patio at a favorite French café finishing our dinner. *What will the future hold?*

I enjoyed assisting Tom on the "Joni" film publicity project, but I wanted to be more than a co-worker. I wanted to be his partner in life.

Our evening with Neil and Cora a week ago had been such fun, and it seemed to have affected Tom, too. Suddenly he seemed more open to the idea of marriage; being with the Logsdons had led him to wonder about where he would be at sixty-five.

He'd even offered to extend my "three-month contract" until Christmas. This contract thing was so crazy! Why did I even put up with such nonsense anyway? Most other girls would have said "adios" long before this point. But something compelled me to hang in there with him.

Many of Tom's actions showed he cared. Three weeks ago he had surprised me with a bouquet of flowers and a beautiful dinner at a little Italian restaurant. After a romantic evening together, he had whispered, "Ginny, I love you so much." I had melted inside. But by the following day, he had packed away his heart and flipped on his analytical computer. He had changed his mind *again*—and was back to being "in like" with me.

But in spite of Tom's indecision, this had been the most wonderful summer of my life. No one had ever treated me as royally as Tom, and I'd never met anyone more thoughtful and considerate. Even when he was only going to be a few minutes late in picking me up, he'd call so I wouldn't worry.

I'll hang in there for now, I thought, *and see what happens*. After all, I had nothing to lose, and everything to gain. And in the meantime, I'd pray like crazy.

But we're still worlds apart, I thought, as we continued discussing what had become the topic of the evening: Tom's healing.

"I believe God has promised to deliver me from my MS, Ginny," Tom declared. "I'm praying it will happen soon."

I was silent. I wanted Tom to be healed, and yet I was so afraid! If God healed Tom, maybe he wouldn't want anything to do with me anymore. If he could run on the beach and play tennis again, why would he want to be saddled down with someone like me? God had never promised *me* a physical healing. I knew I'd never be able to do those things.

"And I'm praying for God to heal you, too," he went on, his expression taking on an air of confidence.

"That would be wonderful," I said half-heartedly, recalling stories of people who had been so preoccupied with their quest for physical healing that they'd missed a lot of what life had to offer.

"And you know what, Ginny? When God does heal me, I'm going to become an evangelist and travel all over the country telling others of God's power."

If I were to marry Tom, I asked myself, *would I want that kind of life?* I bristled inside at the thought of traipsing around from one place to another, bedraggled and exhausted. I enjoyed sharing my faith and my music with others, but I knew I'd never be able to keep up with Tom. I'd wear out quickly trying to go at his pace.

"According to the book *Please Love Me*, " I cautioned him, dumping my truckload of frustration, "the demands of ministry are pretty grueling. Remember how the heroine reached the point of total exhaustion and burnout trying to keep up with it all?" I blurted out, not letting him get a word in edgewise. I was feeling frustrated and upset. "I've heard a lot of stories like that. And it's not going to be me, that's for sure!"

"But Ginny, it might be God's will . . ."

"God's will?" I said angrily. "It's God's will for us to live balanced lives. We don't have to do *everything* to be of value to God and others."

This time Tom was silent. *We're so different*, I thought. *Maybe we're too different*. Tom loved to be on the go; I enjoyed my quiet life. Tom wanted to be healed; I was content to live within my limitations.

"Tom," I said quietly, regaining my composure, "because my strength is limited I try to be especially sensitive to the things I feel God is calling me to do. Then I concentrate on doing those things to the best of my ability."

As the waitress cleared away our dishes and brought the check, I sat mulling over our dinner conversation. Different as we were, I was still very much in love with him. *How will it all turn out?* I wondered.

Back in the car, I leaned my head against Tom's shoulder. The thought of losing him was more than I could bear. "I'm so afraid," I admitted honestly, wiping away a stray tear, "that if God heals you, you won't want to be with me anymore."

Putting his arm around me, he gazed at me with a compassionate, yet distant, look in his eyes. "Ginny, you shouldn't be worried about that. God may never heal me. And if he does . . ." his voice trailed off.

He held me close. I knew he enjoyed being with me. He would tell me often that he liked me and thought I was the most wonderful girl he'd ever known. But I also knew there was nothing I could do to win his love. God would have to help him work out his uncertainties about me. It would take a miracle.

Driving back to my apartment, Tom was unusually quiet. I knew he must be doing some serious thinking.

"Ginny," he began, as he pulled up in front of my building. "I think we shouldn't see each other for a week or so. I need some time to think, to sort things out, to be alone and listen to what God might be trying to say to me."

It was difficult for me to hear those words. But I knew Tom was right in wanting to "wait upon the Lord" for his direction. Thoughts of the fun times we'd shared raced through my mind. *Will we ever have times like those again?* I wondered.

That evening I sank to my knees beside my bed. With tears streaming down my cheeks, I prayed, *Oh, Lord, it seems so impossible that Tom will ever love me as much as I love him. I know there is nothing humanly possible I can do to earn his love. Only you can make the miracle of love grow in his heart, if that is your plan for me.*

As I knelt by my bed sobbing, I ached with the thought that I might never see him again. But I knew I could do nothing better than to commit our relationship to God.

The next day at work I felt alone. I knew God was in control and that he would work out his perfect plan for me, yet I was restless and anxious, lacking in faith. I wanted all the answers now.

All day I tried to be strong, struggling to keep a lid on my emotions. But as I poured myself an afternoon cup of coffee, the tears suddenly began to flow again, uncontrollably.

Then Horatio, our lab director—a cheerful and handsome man—entered the break room. "Virginia, what's the matter? What happened? Why are you crying?" he asked, placing a gentle hand on my shoulder.

I was so embarrassed. I'd never lost control in a public place before. "Oh, it's nothing," I stammered.

"Nothing? You're not crying like this about nothing. Tell me what's wrong? Did something happen here at the lab?"

"N—no. It has nothing to do with the lab," I replied, reaching for a Kleenex. "It's about . . . Tom."

"What about Tom? What happened?"

"Well, yesterday we had a long talk and—" The words caught in my throat.

"And what?"

"I'm so afraid that if God heals Tom he won't want to see me anymore," I blurted out.

"What makes you think Tom is going to be healed? That's a pretty unusual thing."

"He went to a healing service awhile back—and he believes God is going to heal him of his MS."

"Well, if he's the kind of guy who would get healed and then not want to see you anymore, then it's better for you to find out now instead of later, right? You don't want someone like that, do you?"

I shook my head.

"Did he tell you he wouldn't want to see you again if he were healed?"

"No," I said, shaking my head again.

"Then don't worry," Horatio reassured me. "Just wait and see what happens. Give it some time."

I knew he was right; only time would tell. I had to trust God with the outcome.

16

Love's Surprise

Tom

Time's running out, I thought, as I fastened my seat belt and prepared for landing at the Orange County Airport. I was returning from a trip to Bechtel's corporate headquarters in San Francisco, but it wasn't a business deadline I was worrying about.

The summer was almost over and my relationship with Ginny had reached a turning point. I thought back to the night we met and how important that first hug had been to her. I had sensed then that she was lonely, that befriending her might be a mixed blessing for both of us. Now everything was coming to a head.

There seemed to be no permanent place in my life for Ginny. My career, my healing, my future in general, all precluded that. She was naive about the rigors of the business world. You didn't tell your boss you couldn't stay late to update an assignment because your girlfriend was having you over for dinner. He expected perfection—yesterday.

My healing, if it came, couldn't include Ginny either. How could I proclaim the Lord's healing message if Ginny

wasn't healed, too? Of course, the assumption that my healing was imminent certainly wasn't spoken by God. It just
seemed to make sense to me.

And marriage was a third thing that didn't fit into my
plans. I had places to go and things to do. I'd been to several
beautiful weddings with Ginny this summer, but none of
the couples included a handicapped person.

What if I wasn't healed and instead got worse? I couldn't
ask Ginny to take on that risk. As much as I liked—admittedly, even loved—her, our friendship had been doomed
from the start.

Ginny's definition of love was different from mine. When
Ginny said she loved me, she meant she wanted to marry
me and spend the rest of her life with me. It was such an
innocent love! Potential problems didn't seem to enter into
her considerations. She'd even cried when I'd suggested
that I needed time to evaluate our situation.

That's when I knew I was hurting her, that she was too
fragile for me. Those "friendship" contracts had raised her
expectations beyond my intentions. To me, they were
promises to be a friend to a sweet but lonely girl who wasn't
the type to go out looking for dates. Although she was
terrific and I enjoyed holding her close, I controlled my
affection. I knew how volatile and destructive passion could
become—my pre-Christian memories warned me of that.
Love without commitment was too big a gamble.

Suddenly my eyes filled with tears as I screamed silently
at myself, *You built this beautiful girl up, knowing it was impossible—that you could* never *be more than a friend to her.*

Oh, Lord, I prayed, *please bring Ginny a Christian man to love
her, even this week while we're apart. She's so special. Don't let her
be hurt by my friendship.*

*Tom and his best friend Hugo
at Bechtel Power Corporation
1980*

As the passengers began to exit, I looked at the floor, avoiding their glances. I felt waves of despair overwhelming me. *Show me what to do, Lord,* I silently pleaded. *Please show me.*

But no divine revelation came.

The next morning at Bechtel, as I was sitting in my cubicle preparing my trip report, Hugo came by and peeked over the partition.

"Hey, where you gonna watch the game tomorrow?" he asked.

"I really haven't thought about it."

"I can't believe it—not thinking about the 'SC game? You must be in love," he teased.

"What do you mean by that?" I asked defensively.

"That sweet girl, Ginny, you introduced us to last weekend. You stop coming by the boat, date her all summer without telling your best friend until Labor Day, and now you're passing up an 'SC football game on T.V. and a free meal at our house."

"You never invited me," I protested.

"That's never stopped you before. Ellen told me to invite Ginny—and she can bring you, if she wants to," he laughed, walking away with a big grin.

Hugo had been my best friend for eleven years. He had dedicated his Doctoral thesis to me as "a friend who has become almost a brother . . . who convinced me not to give up." He had even visited me all but six of the fifty days I'd been in the hospital during the early stages of my MS. It was no surprise that he and Ellen had been my first Bechtel friends to meet Ginny.

I spent the evening doing laundry and cooking a T.V. dinner. I'd often joked that perma-press shirts and T.V. dinners made marriage unnecessary, but now I wondered. In the beginning I had worried that people would think I couldn't do any better than a handicapped girl. But Ginny's captivating smile and warm personality won hearts everywhere we went. A new thought entered my mind: *If people were thinking I couldn't do any better than Ginny, it wasn't because she was handicapped, it was because she was the best!*

Lying quietly in bed, I listened for what God might be trying to say to me. In the past there had been times when God had spoken to me through another person. Had God been speaking to me through Hugo this morning? Sometimes Hugo seemed to know me better than I knew myself.

Suddenly, I realized that three days apart from Ginny were more than enough. *I don't want to go to Hugo's alone tomorrow night,* I thought. *I'll call Ginny tomorrow morning before she leaves for work.*

What would the future hold? Did I really want God to bring another Christian man to Ginny? Or was I the man I'd prayed for?

17

Don't Limit God

Tom

A week later I took Ginny to her first 'SC game.

"This is our biggest date ever, Ginny," I said, as we sped along the freeway toward the Coliseum.

"It is?" she asked, smiling like a kid about to get a new bike.

"You're about to become a USC Trojan—'SC rules in college football, you know."

"They do?"

"Oh, Ginny, what am I going to do with you? You've got a lot to learn about football. I think you were the first person I ever met who had never even *heard* of Monday Night Football," I teased her.

"But your colors are partly right—burgundy slacks—just like mine." I was thrilled to see her trying to get into the spirit of the game. But with her white, turtle-neck top, she was dressed more feminine than football.

"Well, you said the Trojan colors were cardinal and gold. I hope the gold in this shawl counts, too."

Soon after we got off the freeway we began to see people—dressed in Trojan colors—heading for their pre-game get-togethers. The excitement of another fall football season was in the air.

"Is the parking far from the stands?" Ginny asked. "I've never been to a game at the Coliseum."

"Handicap Parking is only about seventy-five yards from the entrance," I told her, realizing as soon as I said it that "only" was a relative term. Seventy-five yards of walking for Ginny was like a half mile of rolling for me. I could see that using my passes at Trojan games was going to be more difficult with Ginny along. It was hard enough rolling myself all that way, and now Ginny was going to need a ride, too.

"Maybe we can find someone to push us, with you riding on my lap," I added. Suddenly my independence was being threatened. With someone else's needs to consider, life was becoming a lot more complicated.

Getting Ginny to the restroom would be another challenge. My catheter and leg bag gave me control over my rest stops, but Ginny could be another story. With mobs of people to contend with and her difficulty in walking, I would probably have to give her a ride there on my lap. Visions of having to leave at a critical point in the game and missing the key plays raced through my mind. Bringing her to USC games was not going to be easy. An ongoing relationship with Ginny would definitely slow me down. Would it be worth it?

But in spite of my concerns about Ginny slowing me down, the best thing about the game was being with her! We were different in so many ways, yet her warmth and sweet spirit drew me to her.

At halftime we left the game and headed directly to the airport. I had another energy conference in Chicago and needed to be there first thing in the morning.

"I appreciate you dropping me off, Ginny," I said as we pulled up to the American Airlines terminal. "I hope you're not going to get home too late."

"Oh, I'll be fine. It's only 9:00. Are you sure you don't want me to come in with you?"

"I'll be O.K.," I said, leaning over to give her a kiss. "You've walked far enough for one day."

"Have a good trip, Tom. I'll miss you," she said wistfully.

"I'll miss you too. Drive carefully."

Sliding my wheelchair out of the car and onto the street, I climbed into it and waved good-bye. Looking back I saw Ginny lingering in the middle of the loading zone, watching as I rolled up to the terminal entrance. I waved one more time, and finally she pulled away.

On the airplane I mulled over the events of the past few weeks. Ginny had become not only my best friend, but clearly, I'd fallen in love with her. I'd had plenty of girlfriends in the past, but none so special as Ginny. Her own limitations made mine seem less significant, and her strengths were an inspiration to me. I was confused about where our relationship was going, but what we'd shared up to this point had been nothing but pure gold.

After three days at the energy forum in Chicago, I flew to Orlando to visit my newly-discovered mother again. We spent three quality days together—shopping in the air-con-

ditioned mall and just going out to eat and talk. Little by
little, Mom and I were making a dent in the wall that more
than thirty years of separation had built up between us.

On Friday, we drove down to Old Orlando for the Oc-
toberfest. There was a festive spirit in the air. Women
dressed as country maidens and farmers in bib overalls
filled the streets with laughter.

"These carnival games—with the barkers in their wide-
brimmed stetsons—almost make me feel like I'm at a Grat-
wick Firemen's Picnic back in North Tonawanda," I
reminisced.

"Well, Tom," Mom said, pointing down the road. "Look
what's coming next."

I turned just in time to see two young girls in short skirts
and green striped knee socks carrying a banner that
proclaimed boldly, MARTINSVILLE, NEW YORK. Behind
them marched a band of about twenty chunky men in short
leather britches and knee socks, playing tubas and trumpets.

"Umpa! Umpa! Umpa!" their instruments boomed out as
they trooped past us on the old cobblestone street.

"Mom! Martinsville is right next to North Tonawanda!" I
said, tugging at her purse as she watched them pass.

"I know that. Don't forget, I used to live there, too." It had
completely slipped my mind that she had lived within fifteen miles of me for the first ten years of my life. "That's
why I thought you'd enjoy coming here," she said. "But let's
get something to eat. I'm starving."

After ordering our hamburgers and getting settled at a
table, Mom asked, "How's your love life, Tom?"

"I'm still dating Ginny, the girl I met just before I came out
here in June," I explained. "She's very sweet, and I think she
likes me a lot."

"Oh, that's nice," she said, with a big smile. I could see a
twinkle in her eye that seemed to be saying more. After all,

she had two career-oriented bachelor sons who had no apparent plans to keep the Carr name alive by bringing her a grandson.

"Whoa. The chance of my letting her—or any other girl for that matter—get serious with all the uncertainties of my MS is pretty remote."

"Why do you say that?"

"I've seen too many marriages end in divorce. The stress of that kind of situation would probably cause my MS to get much worse. I think I'm better off staying single."

"I've seen some that didn't work out too," she said, taking my hand. "But just remember, Sweetheart, trust and respect are the keys to a lasting relationship, not the physical or material things."

The next morning as I was about to leave, Mom gave me a book titled *Don't Limit God* to read on the plane. It was about an Orlando man whom God had healed of MS. The book told of how he was half dragged, half carried into a miracle healing service where the power of God instantaneously healed him.

As I put the book down, I began to think. The man's experience sounded so much like Becky's. Both of them had received their healings in the twinkling of an eye after confessing their sins and meditating on the same Scripture, James 5:16: "And the prayer of faith shall save the sick and the Lord shall raise him up."

Becky's other key verse had been Matthew 8:17, where Jesus fulfilled the prophecy of Isaiah: "He took our sicknesses and bore our diseases." And the Lord had given me Hebrews 11:1: "Faith is the substance of things hoped for, the evidence of things not seen." Everything seemed to be right. I believed the Word of God and its promises, I'd seen other people who'd been healed of MS, and people like Ginny and my Mom were praying for me. I believed that

God wanted to heal me too. *Surely today, on this plane, in this hour, my physical healing will appear,* I began to think.

Suddenly a tall slender flight attendant, with an apron around her waist and a serving cart in front of her, interrupted my concentration.

"Would you like some lunch, sir? We have ham, turkey, or beef croissant sandwiches," she announced.

"No, thank you. I'm not going to eat right now," I replied.

"How about a big red apple?"

I shook my head and politely waved her off. I had resolved to spend the rest of this flight praying and fasting, beseeching God to let my healing be revealed.

My thoughts drifted back to that Mario Murillo healing service in February. *Did God really speak to me? Did He promise me a physical healing that night? Will it happen today?* I could feel Satan answering "No, no, no" to all my uncertainties.

Oh, Lord, I give up, I cried. Then James 4:17, the verse from a plaque Ginny had given me, came to mind: "The effectual fervent prayer of a righteous man availeth much." *Oh, Lord, I prayed, forgive me for the hardness I've held in my heart toward Mom all these years. I know I can never repay her for the pain and loneliness I've brought her. But, Lord, her only wish is that I be well. Please answer both our prayers.*

Truly I wanted to be healed. Sending the signal from my brain to innervate my leg muscles, I waited for my body to stand. I could feel the nerves giving their marching orders. Would the muscles listen? As they began to tingle with excitement, I could feel new life filling the dormant pathways. My toes strained to tap and wiggle. My calves, once firm and muscular but now flaccid, were being activated.

I pushed my strong arms against the chair, raising my body off the seat as I tried to straighten my legs and stand. But instead they buckled and threw me back on the arm of the chair.

Try again, I thought. *My physical healing is going to take place right here—now, as I pray on this plane.*

But as I sat there waiting for my legs to lift me up, I felt God speaking to my spirit. "Ginny is your healing," he seemed to be telling me.

Suddenly I knew it was true. All the problems with my MS—using a wheelchair, bladder infections, fatigue, the uncertainty—were insignificant to Ginny compared to her love for me.

Her love is like God's love, I thought. *It's unconditional. She accepts me totally—shortcomings and all! The only things she cares about are that I return her love and continue my daily walk with the Lord.*

Through tear-filled eyes, I looked down at my lifeless legs. *Could it be,* I wondered, *that the healing I believed God had promised me was not to be a physical one . . . but an inner healing . . . through God's love and Ginny's love and acceptance of me?*

Yes. I *was* the Christian man I had prayed for God to bring into her life; and she was the healing God had promised me.

18

A God of Miracles

Ginny

Who will I find at the airport this evening? I wondered as I drove toward Los Angeles International to meet Tom. *Will it be the warm and charming man whom I love? Or will it be detached, businesslike Tom?* My emotions fluctuated between excitement and despair as I anticipated seeing him again.

As I thought about it, I realized everything that had happened in the past three weeks pointed to how much Tom did care. He'd even called me twice from Chicago this week.

Was I afraid because it seemed too good to be true? Were my own insecurities keeping me from believing he really loved me? I couldn't bear to think of the pain I'd feel if things didn't work out. But Tom only wanted a convenient "friendship contract," and I wanted to make a lasting commitment. *Our relationship can't continue this way much longer,* I sighed.

Then I remembered my prayer on the afternoon of our first date. I had begged God, *Oh, Lord, please help me to win Tom's heart.*

How foolish, I chided myself, *to think that I could win Tom's love.* Just as God's love couldn't be earned—it's a free gift—I knew there was nothing humanly possible I could do to win Tom's heart either.

Lord, I prayed silently, *you are a God of miracles. And it will take nothing short of a miracle to settle Tom's heart on me. I give Tom to you. I don't even want him anymore, unless you want us together. Please, Lord—right now—place in Tom's heart whatever feelings you want him to have for me.*

Even though I knew I might be giving up all I'd ever hoped for, a wonderful peace spread over me. I was no longer anxious or afraid. The outcome was in God's hands. He alone knew the future. I could trust him to work out what was best for me—and for Tom, whatever that might be.

19

The Ultimate Question

Tom

The 747 finally touched down on the runway, six hours after leaving Orlando. I was bursting with excitement at the thought of seeing Ginny again. It had only been a week since I'd been with her, but my new desire for our relationship made it seem like months.

As I sat in my seat, watching the other passengers clear their overhead luggage racks and walk to the front, I began to wonder: *What if she didn't share my transformation?* Maybe she'd want to wait, to put my proposal on hold. Surely that would make sense. I had been so unpredictable in the way I treated her. It was so easy to be warm and loving with her, tenderly kissing the tip of her nose; she'd sparkle with the innocence of a child searching for her present under the Christmas tree. But when I'd sense she was expecting something more than a casual friendship, I'd pull away and change the subject.

In the beginning she'd wanted my companionship more than I wanted hers, but now the tables had turned. She'd become irresistible to me, and I longed to win her heart.

As I left the plane and traversed the terminal toward the lobby, old doubts began to creep back in. Why did they keep haunting me like this? Could a handicapped woman like Ginny be a functional partner for me? Would she have the ability to do things that I couldn't? Would she fit into my career? Would she be able to be what the Bible calls a helpmate? Or would I end up taking care of her?

It was a mystery to me how Ginny could even take care of herself, let alone a husband. I still remembered how hard my year on crutches had been. How would Ginny—who not only walked with crutches but also with severe scoliosis in her back—be able to shop, carry the laundry, and cook on a regular basis? Indeed, she admitted she hardly ever cooked for herself; that fancy quiche she'd prepared had been an exception to her normal "drive-thru, fast-food" routine. She wouldn't have the energy to cook like that every night.

Suddenly, visions of take-home Kentucky Fried Chicken and Jack-in-the-Box candlelight dinners *for two* raced through my mind. Actually, as I thought about it though, it would be an improvement over take-home or T.V. dinners *for one*—without candles.

Then with new resolve, I said to myself: *With God's help we'll find a way. We'll make a way. After all, didn't God just tell me to marry her?*

Continuing down the long jetway, I strained to catch a glimpse of Ginny. I was so anxious to see her. My stomach churned excitedly at the thought of being with her.

Finally, as I entered the bustling baggage claim area, I spotted her. "Ginny, Ginny! Here I am," I shouted. "I'm coming. Just stay there."

Her face exploded into a broad smile as she turned toward me and waved with her right crutch dangling in the air. I hurried toward her, my heart pounding. *Tonight*, I thought, *we'll both be on the same wave length.*

"Ginny, I'm so glad to be home and to be with you again," I said, near tears. I pulled her close and kissed her tenderly. Her lips felt so soft and warm against mine. As I held her there in my arms for a moment, I suddenly realized how precious she was to me. *For the first time in my life*, I thought, *I'm really in love.* I wanted to shout it out for everyone to hear.

Leaving the terminal, I eyed her peach-colored jumpsuit. "You look especially beautiful tonight, Ginny," I said softly. "Is that a new outfit?"

"In a way it is," she said grinning. "I bought it awhile back and I've been saving it for a special occasion. I'm glad you like it."

"I've missed you so much," I said, as we headed toward the car.

"Wow! I've never heard you talk like this before, Tom. What happened to you in Chicago?"

"It wasn't really Chicago, or even Orlando with my Mom, but something *did* happen to me on the plane about an hour ago. I guess I'd have to say it was a miracle. Let's go to dinner, and I'll tell you all about it."

"Okay," she said, looking puzzled but delighted.

As we lowered the convertible top and drove toward the Pacific Ocean, I planned my strategy. A romantic restaurant overlooking the water would be just the place to pop the question.

A few minutes later, we pulled into Marina Del Rey. After parking the car, I held her again, lingering to watch the splendor of the setting sun on the horizon. The alluring aroma of fresh, mesquite-broiled seafood mingled with the cool ocean air.

"I've really missed you, Ginny."

"Well, I've missed you, too," she said, snuggling a little closer. Without the wheelchair to separate us, her petite body fit perfectly into my arms. The setting seemed ideal, and my pulse raced.

"Hey, beautiful! I skipped lunch on the plane today so we could share a fancy dinner tonight," I said, trying to contain my emotion. "Let's go in and check out the restaurant."

The restaurant offered the typical California steak and fresh seafood cuisine. Rustic lanterns and seascapes of magnificent old sailing vessels that looked as if they could sail right out of the wall highlighted the mariner motif. Through the window, I watched a fishing trawler unloading at the dock. Two burly, unshaven fishermen in worn dungarees were removing an open box of fishing tackle and what looked like a bucket full of fish.

"Well, Ginny, I think the seafood here is fresh," I quipped, motioning for her to look out the window. "They're probably bringing that catch in just for you. This must be your special night."

"Just being here with you makes it special," she answered, her eyes sparkling. Butterflies swirled in my stomach, and I wondered again at the miracle of this beautiful woman seated across the table from me.

The waiter took our orders, and I pondered my next move. Should I tell her what happened on the airplane? Or did I need more time to organize this project? Perhaps I should wait until the next time I saw her. That would give me a few days to reconsider my proposal, to pray and ask God for confirmation that he really wanted me to marry her.

Maybe I was just imagining that God had spoken to me on the plane. *Is it really his idea, or mine?* I still had so many questions.

"Tom, is something wrong? You're not eating," Ginny reached over to touch my hand. My spinach salad, piled high with croutons and covered with hot bacon dressing, sat untouched.

"No, I've just got a lot of things on my mind. That was a long trip, and it's really affected me and my relationship with you."

"What do you mean?" she questioned, her expression turning grim. "Did you meet—another girl?"

"I guess you can say that. But it's not what you think." Taking her hand in mine, I groped for the right words.

Ginny's eyes searched my face for clues as to what might be coming next. Her sparkling expression had turned pained and anxious.

"Ginny, I did meet another girl in Chicago. And she went with me to Florida to visit my mom and then she flew back on the plane with me," I admitted.

A look of sadness and hurt spread across her face. "What are you talking about? You got off the plane alone, and you're being sweeter to me than you've ever been before. I'm all mixed up!"

"I won't keep you guessing, Ginny. I really *did* meet a new girl in Chicago. And I've fallen head over heels in love with her," I said, unable to maintain the charade any longer. "And you know what? She's been my best friend for the past four months. And now I want her to be my wife."

Tears rolled down my cheeks as I reached for Ginny's hand. My heart was pounding so loudly I thought everyone in restaurant would hear it.

"Ginny, I know I haven't always treated you as well as you deserve. I should have called you more and complimented you more and brought you flowers more often."

Then all my pent-up feelings for her gushed out like the falls at Niagara. "My affection for you has been growing with every date we've had. You've become my best and most trusted friend. As I looked at other girls at the conference, none of them could compare to you. And I finally realized that you're the woman I've been looking for all my life. I just hadn't recognized you. You're everything I've ever dreamed of, Ginny."

She gazed back at me in unbelief, her eyes glistening. She seemed to savor every word. I'd been so unpredictable in the past. Would she believe me now?

"This time," I went on, "I'd like to extend our 'contract' to a lifetime. I want you to be my wife, Ginny. Will you marry me?"

Her eyes filled with tears. I knew this was the moment she'd been waiting and praying for all her life. But would I, a man with a progressively disabling disease, fit the part and be able to fulfill her dream? Would she accept me as the answer to her prayers?

20

Is It for Real?

Ginny

My mind raced as I tried to put it all together. Tom had just asked me to marry him.

After waiting and praying that God would work in Tom's heart, suddenly I was filled with fears. I knew the wrong husband could lead to a marriage that would ruin both of our lives.

Is Tom the right man? Or will there be someone else just around the corner?

What if we got married and Tom's MS got worse? Would I be able to take care of him? I knew there were no guarantees in life for anyone; I could marry a perfectly healthy man only to have him be in a car accident—or suffer something even worse. Questions flew through my mind as Tom eyed me, waiting for my reply.

I had only known him for four months. Was that long enough to be giving my life to him? Certainly, I'd dreamed of marrying Tom. But his proposal was so unexpected, *so sudden.* He was asking me to make a lifetime commitment.

Would he feel the same tomorrow? Or would he change his mind and just want to be friends again?

Shouldn't I pray about it first? We'd prayed every time we had been together since the day we met. But did I need to pray more? I had prayed for years that God would allow only the right man to fall in love with me. *Is Tom that man?* I wondered.

What did the "right man" mean anyway? I'd often asked myself that question philosophically. I wanted someone who loved God as much as I did, and who would love me with all his heart for the rest of his life. Of course, I'd also dreamed that my "knight in shining armor" would be tall, dark, and handsome. I wanted him to have a good sense of humor and a real love for people. Tom fulfilled all these criteria—right down to the shining armor of his wheelchair.

Suddenly, I *knew*. "Tom, I love you so much," I whispered, tears streaming down my cheeks. "More than anything else, I want to be your wife."

Silently I asked myself, *Is this for real?* Only a few hours ago on my way to the airport I had prayed, asking God to place in Tom's heart whatever feelings God wanted him to have for me. *What an answer to my prayer!*

As Tom studied my face, his eyes spoke volumes of love. "Ginny, you've made me the happiest man in the world," he said, taking both my hands in his. "I've never felt this wonderful inside before. Thank you for loving me—and for not giving up on me."

I smiled and squeezed his hand. "As my mom used to say, 'perseverance wins.' I guess I've had a lot of practice in that area."

We both laughed. "But what about your healing, Tom?" I said, growing serious again. "You've been praying about it so . . ."

"Oh, Ginny," Tom interrupted, "I was so excited about asking you to marry me, I forgot to tell you about the miracle that happened on the plane. I was deep in prayer, asking God to reveal my healing, when suddenly I heard God speak to me. In a still, small voice, he said—"

"Yes?" I urged. I was sitting on the edge of my chair.

"God told me," he began again, his voice cracking, tears spilling down his cheeks, "that you, Ginny . . . you are my healing."

I could hardly believe my ears as I gazed at him through my own tear-filled eyes. Putting my arms around him, I drew him close. "Tom, I love you," I told him again.

"I guess God knew all along that I needed your love more than I needed physical healing, Ginny," he went on. "I want to slow down and go at your pace, wherever God may lead us." Then he drew my face close to his and gave me a lingering kiss.

As he pressed his lips to mine, we sat lost in our love, oblivious to the world around us.

21
Walking toward Oneness

Tom

I woke up the next morning wondering what I had done. I'd never been willing to consider asking *anyone* to take me on as a life partner, with all the uncertainties of my MS. And yet now, I had asked Ginny, a girl with significant physical limitations of her own, to be my best friend and lover for life. Had God really told me to do it? Or was I just tired at the end of a grueling trip? Hadn't the spiritual gifts tests revealed my gift of celibacy?

When Ginny came over that afternoon, I seized the opportunity to share my misgivings with her.

"How did you sleep last night, Ginny?" I began.

"Great! The best ever in my life," she beamed. "How about you?"

The words spilled out. "Well, I'm kind of worried about last night. I really thought God spoke to me yesterday—about our relationship, I mean—but how can we be sure? I think we should study the Bible together this afternoon and see if it gives us confirmation that we're to be together."

"Oh, Tom, are you going to change your mind again?" she said, big tears welling up in her eyes.

"No. I'm just saying we should read the Bible and pray," I replied, pulling her onto my lap and brushing her tears away with my handkerchief.

"I'd like us to study 1 Corinthians chapter seven."

As I read aloud the entire chapter, verse 35 seemed to confirm what I needed to hear: "I am saying this to help you, not to try to keep you from marrying. I want you to do whatever will help you serve the Lord best . . ."

As I tried to imagine my life without Ginny, I could hardly bear the thought. I had grown to love her so much. And Ginny's love had freed me to love myself and others more than I'd ever dreamed possible.

At that moment, all my doubts disappeared. I knew that having Ginny by my side would not only complement but *enhance* whatever ministry God had for me. I knew God had called us to be together. The fact that our gifts of ministry—mine of speaking and exhortation, and Ginny's special musical talents—also complemented each other was further confirmation.

After Ginny left, I called my friend, Bill, who had always been a source of encouragement to me during the two years we'd known each other. He even attended a men's Bible study every month in my home. I knew he would be interested in hearing the news about Ginny.

"Hi, Bill," I said when he answered the phone. "Have I got news for you!"

"Let me guess. You're up and walking again," he replied, referring back to my March prediction that the Lord would be healing me before Christmas.

"Almost, but not quite—God has revealed to me that Ginny is my healing. On Saturday night, I asked her to marry me. And believe it or not, she said yes."

"Of course I believe it! She's a sweet girl, and you're a great guy. You'll make a wonderful couple. I'm thrilled for both of you."

"I think she's sweet, too, Bill. I know she's not a perfect '10,' but I really do love her."

"Hey, Tom! If you're going to marry her, you better think she's a '10.' You may not think she's perfect, but you better believe she's the ideal girl for you."

As Bill hung up the phone, his words rang in my mind. Obviously, a perfect "10" score was comprised of far more than just physical attributes. Ginny was beautiful, but not like a Hollywood starlet. More importantly, she had a pure heart and was sincere and loyal to me. If anyone in the world could be trusted to love me unfailingly, in spite of my wheelchair and chronic physical problems, it was Ginny. If she could accept me, certainly I could accept her much more minor limitations. Suddenly Ginny's score leaped dramatically over the "10" scale to a MILLION.

A week later we called Ginny's parents in Winona to share our wonderful news with them.

"What do you think your parents will say about you marrying a man in a wheelchair?" I asked, searching her eyes for any sign of hesitation.

"That won't matter to them—they'll just be thrilled that I'm finally getting married," she said jokingly.

I didn't laugh. "I'm not so sure they will. Back in 1973, a month after I left the hospital, I opened the *Los Angeles Times* and read the headline on Dear Abby's column: *Please Help Us Save Our Daughter.*"

Ginny's face grew solemn. "And?"

"The first letter was from a couple whose daughter planned to marry a Vietnam amputee. They told Abby how wonderful their daughter was and what a shame it was that she was going to waste her life married to half a man!" I said, near tears.

"Oh, Tom, what a horrible thing for someone to say!" Ginny's voice was full of indignation.

"Let me finish," I insisted. "Though Abby countered that a physical handicap does not disqualify a man from being a good husband—and she even printed several other letters to that effect the next month—I was not convinced. That letter has haunted me for years, Ginny. I've felt in my heart that no girl's parents would ever accept me."

"But, Tom, my parents aren't like those people. My dad and mom are the most loving and accepting people you could ever hope to meet. And they understand handicaps," she said, putting her arm around my shoulder. "Don't forget, they struggled with my polio. They didn't even know if I would live. And remember, I told you how my dad's leg was mangled in a combine when he was only twelve years old. He had to walk with crutches for years . . . "

"But Ginny!"

There was no stopping her when she got fired up! "And my mom's a nurse," she reminded me. "Believe me, Tom, they don't care whether you're walking or rolling, as long as you're doing it with the Lord."

"Hey, who put the tiger in your tank?" I laughed. "Call them. I'll go pick up the phone in the other room."

A minute later Ginny's voice echoed through the phone, "Hi, Dad."

"H-e-l-l-o-o-o Virginia!" her father answered in his Norwegian brogue. "Are you having a nice day out there in sunny California? Let me get your mother in here, and I'll go to the basement phone."

"Virginia, what a nice surprise," Mrs. Holty greeted Ginny. "We've been trying to call you all day. Were you out for lunch with your friends from the career group?"

"No, I've been out with Tom. We went to church, then out to brunch. He's here with me now."

"Hi, Mr. and Mrs. Holty. I'm Tom."

"H-e-l-l-o-o-o, Tom," her dad chimed in.

"Hi, Tom," Gladys said. "Virginia's told us a lot of nice things about you."

"Well, Ginny's told me some pretty nice things about the two of you, too."

"She has? Uh-oh! What did she tell you?" Gladys chuckled.

"Gladys," Earl Holty jumped in on the other line. "Let Tom talk."

"That's okay. But it sounds like we need a traffic cop with four people on the line all at once," I kidded.

"We'll be quiet," Gladys apologized. "Go on, Tom."

"I don't know how much Ginny's told you about me . . ."

"Well, she told us you're an engineer, and that you've become good friends . . ."

"More than good friends, Mrs. Holty. Ginny's become my best friend. I love her, and I want to ask you both for permission to marry her." I watched Ginny across the room as she smiled back at me.

"This is such a surprise," Gladys stammered. "Virginia told us you were special friends, but—oh, my goodness!"

Ginny looked like she was about ready to explode. "Just say yes!" she blurted out.

"Of course, we'll say yes," Earl broke in. "If Virginia loves you and you're walking with the Lord, that's all we've wanted for any of our kids."

"Well, I'm not exactly 'walking' with the Lord. Did Ginny tell you I use a wheelchair?"

"Yes, she did," Gladys said. "She told us you have MS, but that it's been stable for seven years."

"More or less," I added.

"That's no problem. The Lord will take care of you both." The conversation had now ping-ponged back to Earl in his basement workshop in Winona. Ginny's dad sounded exactly as she had described him—a man of great faith, who believed that "with God all things are possible."

"He's always taken care of Virginia," Earl went on. "When she was just a baby . . ." For the next five minutes, Earl Holty did a proud father monologue about "Virginia," while the rest of us listened. He began with the story of rushing Ginny a hundred and twenty miles to the University of Minnesota hospital when she contracted polio at three years of age. Then he went on to explain how, at four years of age when she was in a full body cast, she'd accepted Jesus into her heart. After recounting some of the highlights of her life, he concluded, "You're a smart man, Tom. Virginia's the best; there's no one else like her in the world." As our conversation drew to a close, it became clear that Earl was much more interested in promoting Ginny and in talking about God's power than he was concerned about my physical limitations.

"We're absolutely thrilled you're going to be our son-in-law, Tom," Gladys added.

As I hung up the telephone and raced over to hug Ginny, I breathed a deep sigh of relief. *Oh ye of little faith*, I thought to myself. For years, God had been preparing the Holty family to embrace me joyfully as their son-in-law. Years of nagging doubts had been finally laid to rest.

22

A Fall to Remember

Ginny

Now that we were engaged, Tom's friend, Bill Foster, recommended that we study the book "Two Become One," a Bible-based studyguide for engaged couples. My response was enthusiastic. I wanted Tom to be the spiritual leader of our home. Since he was a relatively young Christian—compared to me, anyway—it thrilled me to think that we could establish such a routine even before we were married.

Since my apartment was not far from Bechtel, we thought it would be the most convenient place to meet for our study. Although the location was good, the entryway presented a real challenge, to say the least. The only time Tom had been there, my neighbors had carried him down the five steps. But since being independent was important to Tom, I wanted to come up with a way for him to get in without their help.

Looking around, I realized there was another way to get to my building. Tom could come down the back alley driveway, across a grassy area, and through the wrought-iron gate behind the apartment building adjacent to mine. But when I checked with the owner of the building the next day, he informed me the gate lock had been rusted shut for years and could not be opened. He didn't even have a key. So with his permission, I hired a locksmith to saw off the old lock and put on a new one. The new lock cost me thirty dollars! I vowed never to tell Tom. He would think it was crazy for me to go to such extremes.

After the gate was open, I prepared the area further by spraying ant killer on the ant hills. Then I found some old boards and small wooden planks which I placed crosswise over the dirt and grass in the gate area to make it more level. Rather than ask for help, I did it myself. I figured anyone else would probably think the whole idea was pretty far-fetched.

The whole time I was dragging the boards out of the laundry room, I kept thinking: *Tom would just die if he saw me out here doing all this for him. He'd know I was crazy for sure.* But I had promised him he wouldn't have to be carried down the front steps again, that I'd get the back entrance opened. When the last board was in place, I breathed a sigh of satisfaction and relief. My apartment was now wheelchair accessible, and we'd be able to do our study here.

The following evening, as I awaited Tom's arrival, I suddenly heard desperate calls coming from outside. "Ginny! Ginny! Help!"

Rushing toward the back of the building, I found Tom sprawled on the ground. "Tom! What happened?" I cried. I could see he had made it through the gate, but then he'd rolled off the boards. His chair had tipped and thrown him to the ground.

"I fell," he snapped, "and I'm sitting on an ant hill!"

The ants were attacking him at a fearsome rate. They were climbing up his pants and running up his arms. And I was helpless to get him up. *What a disaster this has turned out to be!* I silently chided myself.

"Oh, Tom, let me go get some help," I exclaimed, barely suppressing my laughter at what was almost a comical sight. "I'll see if any of the guys next door are home." There was nothing else for me to do except look for my neighbors. Tom was trapped and unable to move away, and I couldn't get close to help. His overturned chair was wedged against the gate and blocked me on the left side, and the devastated ant hill obstructed me on the right.

Oh, Lord, I prayed as I knocked on my neighbors' door, *please let someone be home.*

"Hurry Ginny!" I could hear Tom shouting in the background, "These ants are eating me alive."

In less than a minute Toby and his roommate appeared at the door with perplexed looks on their faces. When I explained briefly what had happened, they ran ahead of me out to the back. "What happened, brother?" Toby asked as they righted Tom's wheelchair and lifted him back in.

"Can't you tell?" Tom replied, wiping the ants from his arms and brushing the dirt from his pants. "We decided to skip the stairs and take the easy way in, so we wouldn't have to bother you guys. I guess we blew it, huh?"

"Hey, it's no bother to us either way. But the next time you're coming the back way, let us know so we can have our cameras ready," Toby joked.

As Tom rolled into my living room, he barked, "This is crazy, Ginny, absolutely crazy!" His voice resounded with irritation.

I winced but didn't say anything, giving him a moment to cool off first. As much as I wanted to entertain Tom in my beautifully decorated apartment, I realized it was foolish to struggle trying to get him in. Undoubtedly, Tom's wheelchair would never touch the turf at my place again.

"Ginny," he said as we sat down to eat the chicken tostadas I'd prepared, "I don't think this is going to work. If we're really going to do this study, we'll have to do it at my house. I'll be glad to bring home dinner, if you'll come there."

"Oh, Tom, I thought that having you come in through the back gate would be such a good idea."

"You're so sweet," he said, beckoning me to sit on his lap, "and you try so hard. Somehow, I know we're going to make it in our marriage. It may not always be easy, but if we don't take ourselves too seriously and we keep our sense of humor, we're going to have a great life together." As Tom brushed away a stray ant that had managed to survive the ordeal, we both burst out laughing.

Dropping my head on his shoulder, I snuggled up against his chest. I knew why I had fallen in love with Tom. His good-natured disposition and his willingness to forgive quickly were priceless qualities. *How in the world did I ever live without him?* I wondered. I vowed that the ant hill escapade would not be repeated; the next time I tried to help Tom I would try to be wiser and more realistic in my undertakings.

The next week Tom and I celebrated my birthday together—it was my first birthday date ever. Tom surprised me again. After picking me up at my apartment, he drove me around for forty-five minutes, refusing to announce our mystery destination. Finally he stopped at a dinner theater, where we saw "Chapter Two," the play that had opened Tom's eyes to how special I was to him. During the romantic closing scene, the tears in his eyes as he drew me close made this my most unforgettable birthday ever.

Fall had always been my favorite season of the year, but the thrill of being newly-engaged made this autumn extra special. The excitement built even higher the next week when Tom took me to pick out a beautiful diamond, and we left it to be set. As we drove home, I showed Tom the two tiny diamonds, barely visible, on my watch. I'd bought it several years ago, thinking they might be the only diamonds I'd ever own. I could hardly believe that soon I would have my very own engagement ring to remind me continually of Tom's love and commitment to me.

We closed the evening by going to see the public premier of the "Joni" film. The story of her life touched me deeply, but my tears were tears of joy, as I realized that working with Tom to publicize this film was part of the reason we were now planning to build a whole life together.

Leaving the theater that night, I told Tom, "I hope I can meet Joni someday."

"You know what? She's going to be speaking at a hotel near here on Thursday night. Would you like to go? Maybe I could introduce you to her."

"Let's do it!" I replied, thinking how great it would be to meet Joni in person.

It was a big night for me, going to my first banquet with my fiancé. We arrived at the hotel early and were given a table on the periphery, where Tom wouldn't have to contend with chairs blocking his pathway. Then we saw Joni roll in.

"Ginny, wait here, and I'll see if Joni has a few minutes to talk with us before dinner begins," Tom said, turning his chair toward the front. "I don't want you to walk all the way over there and then find out she can't."

I watched as Tom wheeled over to where Joni was chatting with someone at her table. People seemed to be coming from everywhere, and I doubted that it would be possible. But after about five minutes, he returned.

"Joni would love to meet you," he said with a broad smile. So together we made our way over to her table. I could tell Tom was proud to be showing me off. His earlier concerns about my handicap had been replaced by an enthusiasm like that of a sixth grader with a hot-fudge sundae.

"Joni, this is my fiancée, Ginny," Tom said. "We're going to be married next May."

"Congratulations, Tom!" Joni responded warmly, looking from Tom to me. "You're a beautiful lady, Ginny, and I'm so happy for both of you."

"Tom really does make me feel beautiful—that's for sure," I said as I put my hand on his.

"And just to make our engagement official . . . Here's the evidence to prove it!"

Then reaching into his suit-coat pocket, he pulled out a small blue velvet box. As he handed it to me, a wide grin broke out from behind his well-trimmed mustache. All eyes at the table focused on me.

My face felt flushed as I opened the little ring box. "Oooh, Tom," I sighed as I gazed at the sparkling round diamond solitaire nestled inside. Reaching over, I gave him a big kiss.

"Hey, you guys," Joni teased, "you'll have plenty of time for that after next May. Don't forget to pray that I'll be next."

"We will, Joni," I said, taking her splinted hand.

"You bet we will," Tom added. "You're number one on our prayer list—as of today."

"I waited thirty-four years for God to bring Tom into my life, but he was worth waiting for," I said, grinning at Tom. "We know God has someone special out there for you, too, Joni."

23

A Wedding Promise

Ginny

———

The January morning was crisp and clear as my friend Juanita and I set out to shop for my wedding gown. I could hardly believe that very soon I would be a bride. How I wished my mother and sister could be with me to share in the fun. But since they lived too far away, Juanita had agreed to assist me in the many ways a mother would.

Juanita and Harold and their children were almost like family to me. Whenever I couldn't go back to the Midwest to be with my own family for holidays, I'd spend the day with them. Their Scandinavian hospitality made me feel right at home. And the same traditional Christmas Eve aromas— Swedish meatballs, corn pudding, and limpa bread—that wafted from my mom's kitchen also filled Juanita's.

As we pulled up in front of the bridal salon, I told Juanita, "After my sister's wedding ten years ago, I vowed that if I ever got married, I wouldn't have a big wedding like hers. She invited almost three hundred people. It was just too much work. But here I am, sending out almost six hundred invitations for mine!"

Juanita laughed. "What made you change your mind?"

"Ten years of praying, waiting, and dreaming, I guess," I responded with a chuckle. "Tom thought a small wedding at Christmas would be fine. But then we both realized that we had a lot of friends who would want to celebrate this day with us."

"A large wedding can get to be quite expensive, you know," she warned me. "Are you sure you can afford it?"

"I've been saving up for this once-in-a-lifetime occasion for years," I said in my most determined voice. "Believe me, I can afford it. And besides, Mom and Dad will help me with some of the expenses. I want to make this a day we all can remember and cherish for the rest of our lives."

As I fingered through the racks of snowy-white wedding gowns, I reminisced about how my sister and I used to play "wedding" when we were young. We'd dress up in my mother's long, silky, cream-colored robe and rig up a makeshift veil to go with it. Since Marylin was younger, I'd almost always make her be the bridesmaid. How ironic that she'd ended up getting married long before me!

I wasn't the typical bride who went from shop to shop searching for the perfect dress. I didn't have the energy for that kind of thing. Usually, when I saw something I really liked, I'd just buy it. And sure enough, I fell in love with the second gown I tried on.

"I can't believe you made up your mind so fast," Juanita exclaimed. "Are you sure you don't want to try on a couple more, just to be sure?"

I laughed. "Juanita, you're just like Tom. When we went shopping for a china cabinet and dining room set, Tom couldn't believe I fell in love with the first one I saw. He wanted to check out the styles and prices at some other stores, but I convinced him I was thrilled with the one we'd selected."

"Let me get our seamstress," the petite manager of the shop interrupted. "We'll have to make a few minor alterations, but I certainly agree that this dress looks gorgeous on you."

I slid my hand down along the smooth organza and admired the lacy, V-neck bodice. Then I turned around to look at the long French lace train in the mirror behind me. *Thank you, Lord*, I prayed silently, *for putting me in the right place at the right time to find this dress. You knew I wouldn't have the stamina for an all-day shopping marathon.*

The days and weeks flew by as Tom and I made preparations for May 30. I was glad we had decided to wait until May and hadn't rushed into a Christmas wedding. Planning together was fun, and it also gave us lots of practice in learning to function together as a team. Each decision we worked through, though the process was not always easy, gave us a better understanding of one another.

The realization that life would not always be easy came on Easter Sunday, two months before our wedding. We'd spent the day with Tom's sister and her family near San Diego and were on our way home. Halfway back to Fullerton, Tom pulled off the freeway and stammered, "Ginny, I feel light-headed . . . Can you drive the rest of the way? I'm pretty sure I have a fever."

By the time we got back to Tom's condo, he was so weak he couldn't even get out of the car by himself. A neighbor had to help him into the house and into bed. The thermometer confirmed my fears. His temperature was 102 degrees.

I wanted to call his doctor, but Tom kept insisting that he'd be fine in the morning. He told me to go on home, but I was terrified and refused to leave. "I'm going to sleep in the spare bedroom—just in case you get worse during the night, and we need to call for help. I won't leave you here alone."

Although I wondered what his neighbors would think when they saw my car parked out front all night, I thought to myself, *It doesn't matter. I can't leave my sweetheart alone and helpless when he's this sick.*

Early the next morning Tom's temperature was almost 104 degrees—and he seemed confused and incoherent. Now I was really scared. *Why did I listen to Tom?* I chided myself. *He always thinks he's so strong and that he has everything under control.* Well, this time he was wrong. I knew I should have called his doctor last night.

Near tears, I dialed first his doctor and then an ambulance to rush him to the hospital. As I followed the white van carrying its precious cargo to the emergency room, I agonized, *Please, Lord. I love him so much!* I felt so alone and helpless.

"It's a severe kidney infection," his doctor told me. "His MS makes him more susceptible to this type of thing. We'll have to put him on intravenous antibiotics for four or five days." I nodded, numb inside. Already, I was learning the meaning of the vow—*in sickness and in health*—that I was soon to take.

I made daily trips to the hospital to see Tom. On the fourth day, when he was feeling better, I gave him the special gift I'd bought. I watched closely as he unwrapped the package and discovered the words "You Light Up My Life" etched on a wall mirror.

"Oh, Ginny," he blurted out as he gazed first at the words and then at me. "How can I light up your life when I'm here, sick in the hospital? I'm just causing you grief and pain."

Leaning over the bed rail, I kissed him tenderly. "Tom," I said, pressing my wet cheek to his, "I love you with all my heart, and I'm here to stay, for better or for worse. No matter what the future holds, I can't imagine living my life without you!"

Tom drew me close and held me. Then chuckling he said, "And I thought I would be the one taking care of you."

I grinned and suggested, "Let's just agree to take care of each other."

A month later as I sat alone in my apartment writing out my wedding vows, the reality of the commitment I was about to make suddenly overwhelmed me. I stared at the words I had just written: "I will try always to make being sensitive to *your* needs—over and above those of anyone else—a real priority in my life. . . ." Tears spilled out onto the paper as I tried to write, ". . . I promise to stay by your side, no matter what the sacrifice or the cost, all the remaining days of my life."

What would be the sacrifice or the cost? I wondered as I thought about Tom's MS. He'd already told me that he would probably never be able to father a child. But in light of the greater risks involved with his disease, that was the least of my worries. So far his MS had been fairly stable—how I prayed God would keep it that way. But no matter what was in store for us, with God's help, we'd find a way, we'd make a way, we'd manage.

The week before our wedding Tom took me out for a special "last Saturday night as singles" dinner. As we drove up the winding road to the Orange Hill restaurant, my pulse raced in anticipation of the events of the coming week. After years of waiting, our wedding day was just seven days away. All of creation seemed to take on a new brilliance as I heard every bird and saw every flower through the eyes of love.

The hostess led us to a choice corner table with a panoramic view of Orange County. But to my amazement, the centerpiece at our table was even more spectacular than the magnificent hilltop view. Waiting there for me were a dozen long-stemmed red roses arranged in a crystal vase. Leaning over, I took a deep breath, letting their sweet fragrance envelope me.

"Surprise, honey!" Tom said, his eyes twinkling. Then he kissed my hand. "These are for the greatest woman in the world."

"You're so incredible! You sure were worth waiting for," I said, gazing into his eyes. "The only other time I've ever gotten roses was when I was my high school's homecoming queen."

"Now you're *my* homecoming queen," he said, winking at me. "But you haven't seen anything yet."

I watched as he carefully pulled an 8" x 11" parchment out of an envelope and handed it to me. "This is your wedding gift, sweetheart," he said. "It's a poem I wrote for you . . . I spent many hours trying to capture in words how precious you are to me."

Focusing on the words done in meticulous calligraphy, I read the title, "My Wedding Promise to Ginny." As I lifted my eyes to meet Tom's gaze, he took my hand in his and began to read aloud:

I can feel God's love smiling
Through the light of Ginny's face,
Enchanting and beguiling
With every tender embrace.

The setting sun cast a warm glow over us, adding to the romance of the moment, as Tom recited the poem from memory. *My knight in shining armor . . . How could I have ever hoped or dreamed for more than this man?* I thought as I listened intently to his every word.

I'm sure that you can see how
I've become a brand-new man.
The old man cannot be now,
I've been truly born again.

I knew God's love but slightly,
Though I'd read his every word.
I took it all too lightly,
'Til that living voice I heard.

In many ways God can share
Of His purpose for our life,
Through friends, events or in prayer;
For me it's my loving wife.

She has waited on the Lord
Without promise or guarantee,
Keeping her virtue stored
In marriage to be set free.

What God has brought together
Let no man cast asunder.
But every challenge weather
With God's help, preserve the wonder.

Thank you, Lord, for bringing me
Such a jewel for a bride.
Thankful and humble I'll always be
Without any bit of pride.

Please make me the BEST
In her life, like she is in mine,
And give her heavenly rest
And a peace that is divine.

I vow to love and cherish
Ginny, till death do us part.
No earthly thing can perish
The oneness today we start.

24

To God Be the Glory

Tom

"Hey, sleepyhead, wake up or you're going to be late to your own wedding," my brother Jim's baritone voice chided me from the other side of my bedroom door. The clock showed 8:05 A.M. "Mom's cooking up your last bachelor breakfast," he continued, "so you better get out here or I'm going to eat it for you."

How ironic, I mused, as I slowly lifted myself into my wheelchair. Mom was not only cooking my last bachelor breakfast, but in a sense it was almost my first. I had actually known my mother less time than I'd known Ginny. Yet in a matter of hours I'd be publicly declaring that I was leaving her to be joined to Ginny. *Tomorrow Ginny will be rousing me for breakfast*, I thought, as I put on my bathrobe and wheeled out to the kitchen.

"Well, son, are you getting nervous with the big event just a few hours away?" Mom asked, placing a plate of french toast and scrambled eggs on the table. I couldn't remember ever smelling such a home-cooked aroma in my condominium before. Already I was becoming attached to the smells of domestic life.

"Not really, Mom. I'm not the type to get nervous," I replied in a casual voice. "With all the public speaking that I do, this is going to be a piece of cake."

"That *sounds* good, Tom, but don't forget: What you say today stays with you forever," Mom warned.

"Yeah, I know," I gulped, swallowing a bite of coffee cake. "Maybe I'd better start getting nervous."

Leaving the breakfast table, I thought about the implications of what I was doing. Tomorrow my life would no longer be my own. Not only would Ginny be there when I rose in the morning, but she'd be there in the afternoon and evening as well.

My hands were strangely steady as I lifted the razor to shave. That was unusual—I hadn't used anything but an electric shaver in almost a year. If I could get a close, blade shave and eliminate my heavy beard, the wedding pictures would be much better. But if I nicked or cut myself, it could be a disaster. I imagined myself at the altar with a bandaid across my chin. What would people think of that? Slowly and methodically, I completed a perfect shave and joined my brother in the bedroom as he put on his tuxedo jacket.

"Hey, brother Jim. You better be careful! You could be the next to go, looking like the dude you are."

"Well, I've been a bachelor for forty-one years," he responded. "They'll have to be pretty sharp to catch me."

"That's what I thought—'til Ginny came along."

"If you find any more like her, send them back to Buf-falo."

"Ginny's one in a million, Jim. But you keep your eyes open! There are other neat girls around."

When I arrived at the church for picture-taking, Ginny's father—formally dressed in his long brown tuxedo jacket and ascot tie—was standing outside greeting other members of the wedding party. He walked up as we were parking our car, did a pirouette, and proudly waved his tails at me. "How do I look?" he asked. "Do I look like I'm ready to preach if Swindoll doesn't make it to church tomorrow?"

"Sure, Dad. But make sure they tape it, since Ginny and I won't be there to hear you," I teased back.

Rolling into the church I looked down the carpeted aisle decked with flowers and white bows. Large ferns, two large floral bouquets, and seven gold candelabras decorated the platform, transforming it into a garden of colors. No one but the wedding party was here yet, and I wondered how many people would come to share our day. On Sundays, 2500 people filled this sanctuary to hear Pastor Swindoll. But today, only our families and friends from work and our churches would be here. How many of Ginny's meticulously addressed invitations would actually be answered?

My attention was diverted by a group of women in long apricot-colored dresses emerging from a door to the left of the altar. I watched as Ginny's bridesmaids walked out and headed toward the photographer who was setting up his equipment.

Then I spotted Ginny. She looked radiant as she inched along, her long, lacy train trailing behind her. She was the most beautiful bride I'd ever seen. As she waved at me, tears of joy began to wet my cheeks. There was a lightness, a special magic, in her step I'd never noticed before. I was the reason for this beautiful woman's joy.

After an hour of posing, my best man, Hugo, and I went to a side hallway to wait for the processional to begin. We joked about the fun times we'd had when I was a regular part of his family and about the changes to come.

"You won't have to feel obligated to invite me for dinner on Sundays anymore," I kidded him. "When Ginny gets up to speed, we'll have you over to our house."

"Don't worry about that. We'll just have the two of you over. But at least you can start bringing the dessert now," he quipped, giving me a light punch in the shoulder. The look on Hugo's face revealed he was almost as excited about this day as I was.

"Well, Doc." I'd called Hugo that ever since he got his Ph.D. "Did you figure out what you're going to say about us today?" I had asked him to prepare a vignette on our meeting and courtship to share with the audience during the wedding ceremony.

"Of course I did. You gave the right man the job. But I never heard of a best man having to work as hard as I am—taking you up the stairs and speaking—just to get my name on the program," he teased.

"Get ready, men," Pastor Ken—a tall, handsome man—interrupted as he walked into the hallway. "Your time has come."

Entering the sanctuary, I listened as the pianist began the prelude to "Wait on the Lord." Then my friend Margie, in her beautiful soprano voice, began her solo. Diagnosed with Hodgkins disease in her teens, she had been miraculously healed and was now free from any residual effects. Perhaps someday God would place his healing touch on both Ginny and me, too.

The song reminded me of Isaiah 40:31: "They that wait upon the Lord shall renew their strength. They shall mount up with wings like eagles; they shall run and not be weary; they shall walk and not faint." This verse was a favorite of mine. And Ginny and I agreed that it reflected our lives, as we each had waited for God to reveal his plans for us.

As each of Ginny's bridesmaids was escorted in by one of my groomsmen, I grinned and nodded hello. Then, finally, at the back of the aisle, Mr. Holty appeared with Ginny at his side. While the joyful strains of "Jesu, Joy of Man's Desiring" resounded through the sanctuary, Ginny moved carefully down the aisle. She beamed as she walked toward me. I tried to be strong, but I couldn't contain my emotion. This was the woman God had designed especially for me! A torrent of tears ran down my face. Reaching back to grab a handkerchief, I realized that one might not be enough today.

Ginny and I, along with her dad, faced the front of the church while Pastor Ken looked down from the platform. "Thomas, do you take Virginia to be your bride, 'til death do you part?"

Without a second's hesitation, I boomed, "You bet I do!" Ginny's dad looked over at me and grinned while the audience behind me chuckled at my bold declaration. When Ken asked Ginny the same question, she whispered, "I do," and nodded her head.

"Who gives this woman to be married to this man?" Ken asked next.

With a wide smile, Earl responded in his Norwegian brogue, "Her mother and I." Then he gave Ginny a little kiss through her veil and joined Gladys in the front pew. Now it was just the two of us.

During the organ interlude, Hugo came down to take me up to the platform, and two of the ushers carried Ginny up the steps in a stately high-backed chair. This was a first for the Free Church: both bride and groom would sit, facing the audience, throughout the ceremony.

Glancing out into the audience, I was overjoyed to see that so many of Ginny's invitations had been accepted. It especially warmed me to know that all three of my moms— my mother, my sister Jane, and my Aunt Hazel—were with us for our wedding.

The warm glow of candlelight surrounded us as Ginny's friend, Carolyn, sang "Surely the Presence of the Lord Is in This Place." I watched Ginny as she closed her eyes to listen and meditate. *Truly*, I thought, *this song reflects the atmosphere here today.*

Next, Hugo stepped up to the microphone and began. "A little over a year ago, Tom and Ginny met for the first time— in this very church, as a matter of fact. Over the next several months they became good friends but remained quite distant from what one might call a love affair. It took some sound motherly advice on trust and respect, and the value of these virtues, to awaken Tom to the realization that he was falling in love with Ginny."

The audience let out a chuckle, as I sat there grinning at Ginny. Hugo was doing a great job of telling the story. "And when he returned from a visit to his mother in September of last year, he proposed to Ginny."

I glanced down at my mother in the front row. How thrilled I was to have her as part of my life, part of this most important day. I shuddered to think that had I not chosen to honor my mother, God might not have brought Ginny into my life.

"Tom and Ginny's formal engagement was," Hugo continued, "witnessed by Joni Eareckson—author, artist, and friend of Ginny and Tom. I'd like to share a poem from Joni's second book, *A Step Further*, with you now."

"This poem to my mind portrays," he said, his voice beginning to crack, "an important message to us all—and especially to Tom and Ginny's further steps together. Listen as Joni reminds us of the wonderful ways in which God works:

When God wants to drill a man
And thrill a man and skill a man,
When God wants to mold a man
To play the noblest part;
When He yearns with all His heart
To build so great and bold a man
That all the world shall be amazed,
Then watch His methods, watch His ways!

How He ruthlessly perfects
Whom He royally elects,
How He hammers him and hurts him
And with mighty blows converts him
Into shapes and forms of clay
Which only God can understand;
While man's tortured heart is crying
And he lifts beseeching hands!
Yet God bends but never breaks
When man's good He undertakes;
How He uses whom He chooses,
And with mighty power infuses him;
With every act induces him
To try His splendor out—
God knows what He's about!
                                        Author Unknown

I watched as Hugo strained to maintain his composure. He was a great business leader, cool in any situation. But today he was melting.

Then Marc, another friend of Ginny's, began to sing "This Is the Day that the Lord Hath Made." Truly, this was the day that God had been preparing us for.

I gazed at Ginny, sitting there in her lacy white gown. She looked as if she had just stepped out of *Bride* magazine. There was no visible evidence of her handicap. Her crutches were somewhere with her father in the front pew, and her brace was hidden under her long gown. Her sparkling sequined headpiece made her look like a queen. *How blessed I am!* I realized.

Then I began to cry. In the quietness, it seemed as if Ginny and I were here alone. I reached over and squeezed her hand firmly but gently, knowing that she'd always be mine. The irony of the moment struck me profoundly: Exactly a year ago, I had found Ginny crying in this very church. Now the tears were mine—tears of joy.

Pastor Ken stepped up to the microphone again. "Tom and Ginny, there are many handbooks written on marriage, but the best one of all is God's Holy Word, the Bible. God's Word declares that the husband is to be the head of the wife. Not only does this mean that you, Tom, have ultimate authority in the home, but it also means you have ultimate responsibility. You are responsible for the success or failure of the new home being established today. It's an awesome responsibility. You're to be Ginny's protector, her defender, her provider, and her leader.

"But even more than all that, you are to be her lover. We read further in Ephesians 5, 'Husbands, love your wives . . .'

"Ginny's greatest emotional need as a woman is to be loved by the Number One Man of her life. That's you, Tom. At times, you'll not feel like loving Ginny, because at times she may not be lovable. But God commands you to love her. And he's not necessarily talking about feelings; he's talking about a commitment of unconditional love. When you don't feel like loving Ginny, remember that God loves her. Ask God to express his love to her through you—through your personality, your intellect, your body, your emotions. As you begin to implement the actions of love, you will feel a fresh surge of God's unconditional love and passion flowing through you to your wife. Thus you will meet her greatest emotional need in all of life."

I squeezed Ginny's hand as Ken turned to face her. "Scripture has something to say to you too, Ginny," Ken said. "The Bible describes the wife as a helpmeet, a helper suited to her husband's needs. Your real beauty as a woman will be evidenced by that which comes from within. As you allow God to develop those inner qualities in you, you are in effect expressing respect for your husband.

"Tom and Ginny, yours will not be the perfect marriage. There is no such thing . . . because every marriage is entered into by two imperfect people. But as Christians—because you have opened your lives to Jesus Christ—you have his Spirit living in you, enabling you to do virtually the impossible and providing the potential for a happy, successful, fulfilling, and enduring marriage. As you allow God's Word to guide you and his Spirit to enable you, you indeed will build a good marriage," Ken said, smiling at us.

"Even more important than what I have to say to you is what you have to say to each other. The most significant part of a wedding ceremony is the vow—the time when you openly and personally declare your lifelong commitment to each other. We live in a day when vows are thoughtlessly made and readily broken." Ken's expression grew serious. "God's Word reminds us that it is better not to make a vow at all than not to keep it.

"I commend the two of you for having sought God's leadership in your relationship and in the matter of the promises you will make to each other on this particular occasion. You have created your own vows; you have thought through carefully what you are to say to each other.

"Ah, I needn't ask you to join hands—I see you've already done that," Ken chuckled, noting our entwined fingers. "So Tom, you may begin."

"Ginny, Ginny," my voice cracked as I began to recite the vows I'd prepared. "It wasn't luck, but the preordained will of God that we should meet. For the Bible says, 'it is not good for man to be alone. I will make him a companion, a helper suited to his needs.' I accept the joy of becoming your husband, the responsibility of caring for you in your parents' stead, and the privilege of being the only one to whom you will ever give yourself while I live.

"I promise to provide for your bodily needs, to praise and compliment you rather than criticize and complain. I promise not only to forgive you—but also to forget when I feel I've been wronged.

"By the authority vested in me by God's Word as your husband, I promise to lead you as an equal but weaker vessel, to respect you and to build you up in all things, to talk through all of our differences. I promise . . . "

Ginny squeezed my hand and gave me a big smile.

"You like that one, huh?" I said, chuckling. The audience laughed along with us.

"And I promise never to let the sun go down on our anger.

"But most importantly, Ginny, I promise to see you as God sees you, honey, because man looks on the outward appearance, but God looks on the heart. Truly you have a beautiful, beautiful heart," I said, my voice trembling as my eyes filled with tears. "And I promise to make God number one in my life—and Ginny Carr number two."

"As I make God number one in my life, I am more able to love myself and to love you, sweetheart. And Ginny," I stammered, "you've helped me to love myself more in the last year than I ever dreamed possible.

"Ginny, I absolutely promise you that God loves you— and in front of a thousand people—I want you to know that God loves you, and so do I. His Word says, 'What God has brought together, let no man cast asunder.' It was God's idea, not mine, that we get together, but I'm thrilled." Ginny squeezed my hand tightly and laughed, and the congregation also burst into laughter.

Growing serious again, I went on. "And I will never cast it asunder. This is for life. I love you, Ginny, forever and ever. Thank you for having me as your husband."

Ken then turned to Ginny and asked her to give her words of promise and commitment to me. Ginny looked radiant as she began.

"Tom, I love you, and I'm overjoyed that God has brought me to you and that today I will become one with you. I know God has specifically designed me to be your partner, and because of that I promise to seek God's help in being the kind of wife he wants me to be. I will try to make being sensitive to your needs, over and above those of anyone else's, a real priority in my life.

"I promise to comfort you in times of sorrow, to share your joy, and to encourage and assist you in times of abundance as well as in times of stress and want."

She recited her vows calmly without notes or any hint of nervousness. She'd told me the night before that she would have to be strong because if she started to cry, she would never be able to finish. I couldn't believe how great she was doing.

"I promise to keep short accounts with you," she continued, "and never to let the sun go down on my wrath. I promise to trust and respect you, and to reverence you as my spiritual leader and the head of our home.

"Tom, knowing that your love is an extension of God's love for me, I willingly give and submit my life to you," she said, looking directly into my eyes, "promising to share every aspect of it with you.

"Because of my deep love and devotion to you, I promise to be loyal to you and to stay by your side—no matter what the sacrifice or the cost—for all the remaining days of my life.

"Next to the Lord, Tom," she beamed, "my delight is in you. You are the most wonderful blessing God has ever brought into my life. I love you."

After we exchanged rings, Ken gave his closing remarks. "Because God looks with favor upon this relationship, it's my privilege to pronounce you husband and wife, in the name of the Father, the Son, and the Holy Spirit. God's Word says, 'Those whom he has joined together, let no man, let no woman, ever separate.' "

Upon Ken's invitation "to be the first to kiss the bride," I embraced Ginny and gave her a jubilant kiss. Then Ken announced to the congregation, "It's my privilege to present to you for the very first time, Mr. and Mrs. Thomas Lee Carr."

The audience broke into spontaneous, thunderous applause. I could see my mother and sister dabbing their tears in the front row while my brother-in-law, Jim, and my nieces, Ann and Karen, smiled their approval.

After being helped down the platform steps, Ginny slipped onto my lap. Then, like a knight in Renaissance days, I whisked her away. As we started up the aisle with Hugo and Ginny's sister pushing us, Margaret, our organist, let out all the stops and began to play the triumphant strains of the "Hallelujah Chorus" to more enthusiastic applause.

We paused briefly in the narthex, as Marc began to sing "My Tribute," the closing number. The words of the song touched me deeply. Indeed they were my heartfelt prayer to God:

How can I say thanks for the things
   You have done for me?
Things so undeserved, yet You give
   to prove Your love for me.

To God Be the Glory

Tom   ✝   Ginny

May 30, 1981

**For the Lord seeth not
as man seeth;
For man looketh on the
outward appearance, but the
Lord looketh on the heart.**

1 Samuel 16:7

*Tom's family
(l. to r.) mother,
sister Jane,
brother Jim*

© 1981 John Buckle
Photography

*Ginny's family
(l. to r.) mother,
sister Marylin,
Ginny, brother
Dave, father*

© 1981 John Buckle
Photography

Tom and Ginny Carr
Wedding Day
© 1981 John Buckle Photography

25

Only the Beginning

Tom

On our first morning in Hawaii, I sat out on our twelfth-floor *lanai* and scanned the panoramic view of the blue Pacific Ocean. The air was fresh and clean, and the sun glistened on the surf. Ginny and I were excited about our plans for a beautiful honeymoon week in "paradise."

As I glanced through one of the local entertainment brochures, Ginny came up behind me and kissed my neck. It was still hard to believe that after years of bachelorhood, I was actually married to this wonderful woman. But there she was, leaning against the railing, a gentle breeze fluffing her hair.

Her cute yellow sunsuit revealed her bare legs as she stood there, surveying the breathtaking view. Her legs weren't smooth and shapely like a Manhattan Beach bathing beauty's would be. Her right leg, paralyzed by childhood polio, was flaccid; her left leg was small, but firm. As she walked across the *lanai*, I studied the great strength and determination with which her left leg carried her body while her right one dragged behind. I'd always been a connoisseur of fine legs, especially since I'd lost the use of my own. But Ginny's legs were in a class by themselves. They carried the woman I loved.

"Do you mind if I call room service for some coffee?" she asked, as she turned toward me.

"Why don't we just go down and get it in the lobby?" I suggested. "It's complimentary 'til ten."

"I don't think I can make it. It's 9:30 already, and I've still got to put on my brace—and some makeup," she said, looking at her watch.

"Well, go ahead. But it'll probably cost a dollar a cup," I added, as she moved into the room.

"I promise I'll be ready earlier tomorrow," she said, picking up the bedside telephone.

When the room service waiter arrived, I was stunned to hear him say, "Two dollars, please. That's our minimum charge."

I'd heard jokes about how trivial things like not tightening the cap on the toothpaste could lead to marital conflict, and I wondered if our hangup would be coffee. Ginny was a coffee-at-any-price fanatic, and I was a who-needs-coffee tightwad! But as I watched her enjoying her two-dollar cup of coffee, I realized it was a small price to pay for getting our marriage off to a good start.

The following afternoon we encountered our next major challenge—a trip to the International Marketplace. Since it was "only" four blocks from our hotel, I boldly declared to Ginny that she could ride there on my lap. I even encouraged her to leave her leg brace in the room so she'd be lighter to carry.

By the time we arrived there an hour later, I was totally frustrated and exhausted, too tired to enjoy anything except eating a late lunch and resting up for the trip back. Rolling back to the hotel, Ginny used her crutches to help me propel the wheelchair. Amused passersby also assisted us in getting across busy streets and up curbs in what must have been a comic scene.

After that we began taking taxis to go anywhere further than the block to the beach. With less concern about finances, we were able to have a much more relaxing and enjoyable, once-in-a-lifetime honeymoon. We even extended our stay from seven to twelve days, wishing we could have stayed even longer.

The stars were still in our eyes when we returned to my condominium and began merging households. The first weekend, friends moved dozens of packed boxes from Ginny's apartment to my condo—filling the den and guest bedroom, floor to ceiling, with all her earthly possessions. Then we settled into adjusting to our new life together.

For Ginny, the microwave, which my sister's family gave us, was a high point of her new residence. She learned quickly what an incredible time and energy saver it could be. She loved the idea of being able to cook and serve from the same dish, minimizing the clean-up effort.

The dishwasher was another time and energy-saving novelty for her. She had washed dishes by hand all her life and now she'd be able to sit back and give her hands a rest. But first she had to find a way to get my glasses spotless. As a bachelor, I had never minded speckled drinking glasses, but Ginny had a different opinion. Somehow she'd get them clean.

Finally one afternoon, while I was away at work, Ginny hit on the solution. Rather than put the powdered soap in the dishwasher, she would use the trusty old liquid soap that had brightened her crystal for years. She packed the dishwasher full of all the glasses she could find, even those

I alleged were clean enough. Then she filled the soap dispenser with her blue liquid soap and turned on the machine, thinking, *Won't Tom be surprised?*

And surprised I was! When I came home that evening, I found Ginny dressed in her housecoat, sitting in a bubble bath on the kitchen floor. A dozen soaking-wet towels surrounded her. The dishwasher had become a foaming monster, belching suds in every direction.

"Ginny, if this is the way you wash the floor, I think you're trying too hard!" I exclaimed, laughing at the hilarious sight.

She smiled sheepishly. "Honey, did you ever know another girl who could wash the dishes, the floor, and herself all at the same time?" That incident was just another crazy reminder that life wouldn't always be easy, but with the right attitude, we could keep it fun.

A week later, sitting together in my recliner, we discussed our goals, hopes, and dreams for the future.

I told Ginny that for our first year together, I wanted to adopt the Deuteronomy 24:5 philosophy: "A newly married man is not to be . . . given any other special responsibilities; for a year he shall be free at home, happy with his wife." We agreed not to take on any major projects during our first year together. We'd use the time to get to know each other and to build a strong foundation for our marriage.

However, we did establish some five-year goals for our ministry together. The first was to develop a Christian support group for people with MS or other disabilities, where newly disabled people could meet with those who had already gone through the adjustment stage. Two other goals were to make a record and to write a book.

Ginny dreamed of developing her music ministry and making a flute record. My dream was to write a book, perhaps chronicling the lives of some outstanding Christian businessmen.

Our discussion spilled over into our prayers that night and then continued as we lay in bed talking.

"What about children, Ginny?" I asked. "Does it bother you that we might not be able to have any of our own?"

"You're more important to me, Tom, than children or anything else," she said, looking lovingly into my eyes. "I guess I'd always assumed that when I got married I would want children. But my doctor told me that carrying and delivering a baby would probably make the curve in my spine a lot worse than it is already—and taking care of a child might be more than I could handle."

"I think you're right, sweetheart," I said, pulling her close to me. "Between the two of us, we've got enough challenges to deal with. In this day and age, it seems that parenting is an enormous challenge—even for two healthy people."

"I have an idea," she went on, her expression brightening. "When I was in college, I taught a sixth-grade Sunday school class at my church. And as a class, we sponsored a little girl through World Vision.

"Ironically," she continued, "she lived in Hong Kong. And when I went there as a short-term missionary, I was able to meet her. Irene, my friend from the lab, would go along on our outings to interpret for us. We had some wonderful times together."

"So you want to sponsor a child?"

She nodded. "Could we?"

"Of course, I think it's a great idea," I assured her, breathing a sigh of relief that the issue of children could be so easily resolved. *Certainly, God has prepared her for me in more ways than one,* I thought as I pulled her even closer.

"Maybe I could even do a benefit concert," Ginny said, snuggling closer, "or make a record to raise money for orphans someday." Her voice was full of enthusiasm. It was obvious she wasn't spending much time dwelling on the negatives of the situation. She was already dreaming and making plans for the future.

Now when people ask us, "Do you have any children?" Ginny loves to answer, "Yes, we sponsor a young boy through World Vision. His name is Marcos, and he lives in the Philippines."

It warms our hearts to think that we can help build a brighter future for one of the world's millions of hurting children.

26

It Can Be Done—Together!

Tom

Ginny made it through our first several months of married life without using the spare wheelchair I'd offered her on our first date. Although I could see that walking—and especially carrying things like laundry from room to room—was difficult for her, she seemed to find a way to get things done.

But at the end of September, as I was at work boning up for a T.V. interview scheduled for that night, the telephone rang. "I fell and sprained my ankle," Ginny lamented. "I didn't have my leg brace on, and I lost my balance."

That evening at the T.V. studio the staff and camera crew looked puzzled when I rolled in with Ginny on my lap, her foot wrapped in an ace bandage. We must have been quite a comical sight!

The taping session went well, but the comedy wasn't over yet. After the interview, my shoeless wife and I went out to a fancy Hollywood restaurant, with me rolling her in on my lap again. We laughed as people turned and looked our way, joking that perhaps Hollywood nightlife had never before laid eyes on such a crazy twosome. Even the hardship of Ginny's sprained ankle couldn't keep us from having a good time.

For the next five days Ginny used my spare wheelchair. But when her ankle healed, the chair went back in the storeroom, even though she'd seen the ease with which she could get around and conserve her energy. Her pride seemed to keep her from wanting to be seen in the chair—or admitting that it made life easier.

However, Christmas marked the turning point in Ginny's resistance to the chair. Bubbling over with excitement as she handed me a gift, she tripped and sprained her ankle again. This time the sprain was more severe, and she was forced to use the wheelchair for two whole weeks. By the end of the two-week period, she had realized that cooking, doing the laundry, and running our household from a wheelchair was clearly easier than putting on her leg brace everyday and walking around the house with crutches. At last, the wheelchair had become her friend, too.

As much as possible, Ginny still likes to walk whenever we go out, but she no longer lets her pride get in the way when the chair can make things easier. Now she's enjoying places like shopping malls—where distance used to really tire her out—via "her wheels." And together we take hand-in-hand "rolls" along the winding paths at our condominium development, stopping to appreciate the cascading waterfalls and beautiful forest-like setting. The wheelchair has opened up a world of independence—which she never enjoyed before.

In January, over an evening meal, we reached another milestone in our understanding of each other.

"What's this, honey?" I asked as I swirled my fork around in the mushy red mixture on my dinner plate.

"Manna," Ginny joked. "It doesn't have a name. It's a mixture of herbs and leftover chicken and vegetables that I put tomato sauce on. I know how you love tomato sauce."

"Have you tried it?" I asked, sampling a forkful.

"Yes. But it didn't turn out quite like I wanted it to."

Trying to be tactful, I said, "Honey, I think, maybe, *maybe* there are too many herbs in it."

"I know it tastes awful! I was going to try to make something else, but I was just too tired," Ginny said, tears welling up in her eyes. Then she declared, "I knew I could never be a good wife. I don't have the energy to do all the things a wife should do. I get so tired trying to keep up with everything."

"Hey, wait a minute. I thought we were talking about one terrible meal—but this sounds more like an identity crisis. Honey, you're a great wife. What makes you think you're not?"

"I wish I had the energy to do more things for you, to do more shopping so I could cook you fancy meals . . ."

"Stop," I said, reaching over the dinner table and pulling her toward me. "It's not what you *do* that I love, honey. It's who you *are*! You're a fabulous person, and I can't imagine living without you."

"Are you sure?" she said, snuggling up to me as I wiped away her tears.

"Of course. Did you ever hear Ricky Nelson's song, 'Be-bop Baby'? Well, you're my 'Be-bop.' "

Her expression brightened. "Oh, Tom, I love you with all my heart, and you make me feel so loved! But what about this terrible meal? You must be starving."

"Be-bop," I said, gently kissing the tip of her nose, "let's throw this manna away and go to Wendy's for a couple of chicken club sandwiches and a baked potato. You won't even have to put your brace on."

"Thanks, honey," she said, giving me a big hug.

Since then, we've made it a policy to keep a couple of extra frozen dinners in the freezer—just in case.

A year later, two special events took us east for several weeks. Bechtel was selected by the President's Commission on the Employment of the Handicapped as winner of the 1982 "Large Employer of the Year" Award. Ginny went with me to Washington, D.C. to receive the award given in recognition of Bechtel's efforts in training and placing handicapped people during the previous two years. The Bechtel Manager of Personnel Development had said it was my performance that inspired him to institute the program.

Then we flew to Winona, Minnesota, where Ginny's parents had a "year later" wedding reception for us attended by about 150 of Ginny's relatives and friends. And seeing the picturesque Mississippi River Valley where Ginny grew up was an added bonus.

That next summer our dream of having a ministry together also became a reality when we were asked to lead a Special Education Sunday school class at our church. Although neither of us had any experience in working with the mentally handicapped, we felt it was a calling from the Lord. I remember Ginny saying, "Now our full cup of love can spill over to bless others in search of healing love." As Hebrews 13:2 puts it, "Don't forget to be kind to strangers, for some who have done this have entertained angels without realizing it!" Our involvement with these special students has opened up a new world of love and understanding about this unique group of often neglected and misunderstood people.

Then in December of 1982, I received another call from the "It Can Be Done" television program. This time they invited

Ginny and me to make a program about our marriage. Our first date had been the night of my interview for the program two and a half years before. Now they thought a show featuring our romance would make a great follow-up.

So, a second time, we made our way over to the studios in Hollywood. Only this time Ginny was on the set with me.

As the cameras rolled in, Ted—the program's co-host—began, "No matter what the handicap, you can overcome it. Our two guests today have written a book—in pictures. It's a wedding book," he said, flipping through the pages of our wedding album. Here it says: 'For the Lord seeth not as man seeth; For man looketh on the outward appearance, but the Lord looketh on the heart.' Today we're going to show you the product of those who looked on the hearts of each other, found what they wanted, and have been fulfilled thereby."

"Let me introduce you to Thomas Lee Carr and Ginny Lee Holty Carr."

"They had their first date here at KHJ," Mildred, the program's other host, added.

During the first fifteen minutes of the show, Mildred and Ted questioned us about how we'd met. Then portions of our wedding videotape, along with selected photos from our album, were shown for the benefit of the television audience. As we watched the screen, Ginny and I reminisced and commented on the events of our wedding day.

Halfway through the program, Ted turned to Ginny and asked, "What made you so comfortable with Tom? I guess that's the word—*comfort, support*, what a person needs. Did you detect this need in him and set out to allay his fears?"

"When I met Tom and we started becoming friends, I could see that he was afraid of me. He had always wanted to date very beautiful girls—Cheryl-Tiegs-type of girls. I guess every guy dreams of that. He felt people would think less of him if he was dating a girl with a handicap. I could sense he felt that way. He was fighting our relationship, even our friendship, all the time because he was afraid that something more might come of it . . . It was difficult for me to see him struggling like that. But as the months went on, he finally resolved his concerns."

Mildred leaned forward, her eyes filled with compassion. "You must have suffered a lot of insecurity yourself, Ginny."

"Yes, I did. Tom thought I was such a beautiful person, and he would tell me all the time that I was the most wonderful girl in the world," Ginny answered, looking first at me, then back at Mildred. "But he just liked me, and he only wanted to be friends. That was very difficult for me. I prayed about it continually. Each time we went out, I wondered if I'd ever see him again. I didn't know if all those fears would overwhelm him—and he would decide to take off.

"But as I continually committed our relationship to the Lord, God changed his heart. It wasn't me . . ."

"You two have based your relationship on an acceptance of God, haven't you?" Ted added. "Was this something that helped you overcome some of the fears you might have had, Tom?"

I held Ginny's hand securely in mine. "It isn't simply a matter of helping, Ted. I went to see my mother in Florida in September of 1980 and told her I was seeing a handicapped woman. She replied, 'Tom, trust and respect are the most important things in the world.' I got on that plane to come home from Florida, and I prayed that God would heal me of MS . . . I really wanted to be healed physically," I said, my voice beginning to crack. "And God flat out told me, in the way that God speaks to me, 'Your healing is in that girl.'

"I got off the plane and took Ginny out to dinner and asked her to marry me. And I've never been happier in my life! I have peace that God told me to marry Ginny. I'd always thought she was the most wonderful woman in the world, but I was afraid of marrying anyone. And a woman who had a handicap—that *really* scared me."

"But now you're holding onto her with both hands," Mildred noted.

I gazed into Ginny's eyes for a moment. "Oh, you bet! I'm thrilled God told me to do it."

"What about the fears, the anxieties," Ted continued, "when all of a sudden you realized, okay, now we are man and wife. How do you achieve the serenity I see in both of you? Now, Tom, you mentioned *trust* and *respect*. Is that what you base your marriage on?"

"Well, we base it on the fact that we pray together every morning and every night. And we trust the Lord to use our lives as a blessing to others. We're working with developmentally disabled students at our church now. I've done a lot of things successfully by myself, but now we have a ministry together.

"When you bless us with the opportunity to speak to you, we feel it's an opportunity to share the love God's given us."

"Well, you're blessing us by being here, that's for sure," Ted said, nodding his head. "I really don't know quite how to express it. It's an unusual thing to see two happy people, *married* people, in Hollywood, of all places.

"Tom said he was worried about marrying a handicapped woman. Ginny, how did you feel about marrying a handicapped man?"

"When I met Tom—well, he was *special*," Ginny said, squeezing my hand. "I know he has MS, and we don't know what the future holds. His condition is stable and has been for ten years, but we don't know if it's going to get worse in the future or . . ."

"You're in a very remarkable position mentally, however," Ted interrupted, "because you put it in a phrase, 'it'll be the Lord's will.' So you're homefree then, aren't you, if you accept that?"

"That's right," Ginny agreed. "Even if I had married a perfectly healthy man, you never know. He could be in a car accident and be left worse off than Tom. Our lives are totally in God's hands. We believe he will take care of us. And if things get worse, he will somehow enable us to manage.

"We know we are meant for each other and that God brought us together. That's what gives us serenity in spite of our difficulties."

Mildred smiled. "You two were meant to be together."

"That's right!" I said, grinning. "And we're going to have as much fun as we can, as long as we can, and just know the Lord's in it."

"That's beautiful," Ted said as he began his closing remarks. "Tom, congratulations! Ginny, congratulations! May you always be happy, and I know you both will. And congratulations to you folks who have watched these two today. I think they've been one of the greatest inspirations we've had on this program.

"And with that kiss Tom's giving Ginny, I guess we've proved it, haven't we?" Ted declared with a grin. "It's time to say good-bye, but not to your affection . . . May it last forever."

27

Rx for a Priceless Marriage

Ginny

During our first year together we began to learn the importance of working as a team. For example, Tom couldn't reach high enough to change light bulbs, but I could. So on many occasions, I became Tom's hands. And Tom often became my legs—rolling me on his lap when I would get tired from walking. This interdependence has helped to create a strong bond between us and has given us a deep appreciation for one another.

We also determined, early on, not to let trivial differences or anger divide us. We can't afford to waste our energy on small "tiffs"; we need all the strength we can muster just to face the physical challenges of everyday life. And for more serious debates—Tom sometimes teases, "We have no choice but to talk things through; neither of us can move fast enough to get away from the other."

Bringing two physical handicaps into a marriage, along with all the other challenges a relationship faces, has not been easy. But on the other hand, our handicaps have forced us to look beyond the surface to find other things we admire and value in one another. In light of this, the verse we had printed on the front of our wedding program has become especially meaningful to us. 1 Samuel 16:7 reads: "For the Lord seeth not as man seeth; for man looketh on the outward appearance, but the Lord looketh on the heart." God, in his infinite love, has been teaching us to see each other as he sees us.

We are often asked, "What's your secret? In spite of your trials, you two seem to be so happy and so much in love." Indeed, if our marriage appears special to others, it's only because of some basic principles we apply from day to day.

These are the *PR principles*—all beginning with the letters "PR"—which Tom and I have incorporated into our years of marriage. We have found that practicing these PR's has helped to keep our love fresh and growing deeper with each new day.

Prayer

PRayer—daily for and with each other. This prayer time brings a special closeness to our relationship and helps expose hidden wounds that otherwise might go unnoticed. It is extremely difficult to pray together when there are unsettled differences between us.

One night before bedtime I prayed curtly, "Dear Lord, 1-2-3. Amen." I just didn't have the heart to pray when things weren't right between us. Tom knew immediately that something was wrong. We stayed up half the night resolving the conflict, but it was worth the time and effort. When we share our hearts with God, he becomes the intermediary in the dispute.

We prayed together twice on the day we met, and we've never missed a day since we married. Our prayers have been over the telephone, early in the morning, and late in the evening. Our schedules may vary, but our commitment to pray together daily remains steadfast.

In the wedding vows we wrote, Tom and I both promised "never to let the sun go down on our anger." We don't allow things to fester; we are committed to resolving conflicts as quickly as possible. Keeping short accounts with one another, sharing, and praying together has helped us to keep those vows.

Praise

PRaise, through words, thoughts, and deeds, is also a daily part of our walk together. Almost every day when I wake up, Tom looks over at my sleepy eyes and messy hair and tells me how much he loves me. This begins a 60-second debate about whether Tom is the greatest (my opinion) or I am (his contention). It's not a very profound discussion, but it sure is an uplifting way to begin the day. Our praise reflects that we really are each other's *Number One Fan*. And we're not afraid to admit it!

Tom says that if God took him to heaven and then told him he could come back to life with a whole new identity, he'd want to be "Ginny Carr's next husband!" And I love to tell how Tom has become my "knight in shining armor." As we have consistently affirmed each other, our love has blossomed and grown deeper.

Psychologist James Dobson says that the greatest cause of depression for the married woman is not financial trouble, sexual problems, or even in-laws. It's low self-esteem. Men typically work outside the home, where they receive positive feedback from their employers through promotions, raises, and other acknowledgments of their value to the company. However, women at home often receive no recognition for the hard work they put into their jobs. Tom realizes this and tries to affirm my homemaking skills.

In our vows, we made the commitment to "praise and compliment, not criticize and complain." Over the years, we've had many more positive things to praise about one another than trivial complaints to air. Praise helps us appreciate each other more and keeps our relationship in loving perspective. But when we do disagree, both of us are careful not to make any stinging comments which might assail the other's character or self-esteem.

Priorities

What are our *PRiorities* in this hustle-and-bustle world in which we live? Where does our marriage rank in comparison to jobs, hobbies, friends, Bible study, and children? A couple often assumes their marriage will roll along happily ever after without making it a priority. Togetherness may be the most neglected value in the busy American home.

Overcommitment to my music ministry could draw me away from Tom. But we give top priority to invitations where we can share as a musical/speaking team. Since God has blessed us with gifts that complement each other, we delight in serving the Lord together.

Developing and enjoying hobbies together is another way we make our relationship a top priority. Shared activities help keep our interests and our lives going in the same direction.

To make our marriage a priority, we set aside time to be together. We reserve one night a week for each other with no competition from sports, reading, or television. Sometimes we sit in Tom's recliner and talk about the week and any ongoing concerns. We also dedicate every Saturday morning to one another. We take the phone off the hook and do our own thing—together!

Presents
The *PResents* we give each other take on many different forms—gifts of time, energy, material gifts, or actual physical presence. They don't have to be expensive or time consuming; they simply need to reflect the fact that we're thinking about each other and want to do something special.

Tom and Ginny enjoying the view at Forest Home, California
Photo © 1983, Alan Cliburn

I include hand-written "I love you" notes with Tom's lunch during the week. They don't cost anything, but they show him that I prepared his tuna-salad sandwich and carrot sticks with love. And sometimes I surprise him with his favorite drink (a glass of fresh squeezed orange juice) or treat him to a night out. I've found that surprises now and then make Tom feel really special, too.

Tom sends me cards and frequently stops at a street-corner stand to buy me flowers. Six carnations only cost a couple of dollars, but they brighten our home—and our marriage continuously. And one of the most wonderful gifts of time and energy he gives me is his willingness to rub my sore back every night.

A few years ago at Christmas Tom gave me another unique gift. He wrapped the book *What Wives Wish Their Husbands Knew About Women* by Dr. James Dobson and gave it to me with a note saying *he* would read it. This gift will continue to bear fruit for a lifetime.

Thoughtful gifts put our love into action.

Pranks

PRanks—as long as they're harmless—can keep humor in a sometimes too serious situation, applying the medicinal balm of laughter. Dealing with two handicaps in one family creates some incredibly stressful times. We often joke that if we weren't laughing about our circumstances and some of the crazy things that happen, we'd be crying for sure.

Tom's favorite prank is to roll up behind me when I'm engrossed in reading a book or magazine and shout, "Boo!" Then we both have a chuckle as I tell him what a rascal he is! I return the prank by waiting around the corner and startling him as he comes down the hallway. He's harder to catch, but we both get a big laugh when I'm able to turn the tables on him.

Sometimes a bit of humor can even help to quell conflict. When Tom and I are in the middle of a disagreement—and each of us is trying to defend his individual point of view—often, in exasperation, one of us blurts out some crazy comment. Soon we're both laughing. With the tension abated, our conflict is more easily resolved.

A good sense of humor is a great asset to any marriage.

Practice

Like becoming an accomplished musician, a successful marriage requires *PRactice* in order to achieve excellence. It takes a lot of time, patience, and hard work. Partners must rest in the knowledge that it's not always going to be fun and the rewards are not always immediate, but that improvement is sure to come. Even after we learn the principles of how to maintain our marriages, we must continually put them into practice. Emphasizing the positives rather than the negatives can make a big difference in the way we relate as husband and wife.

We all bring scars into our marriages. Tom's and mine just happen to be visible. But invisible ones can be just as difficult. All of us have our own hidden pain. With sensitivity and affirmation, we can help heal the hurt.

Ours is not the perfect marriage, but Tom is more than I'd ever hoped for in a husband, and I can't imagine being happier. Tom and I know we'll continue to have our differences now and then, but together we have resolved not to let any issue loom larger than our love for God and our love and commitment to each other. .

Storybook marriages don't just happen. But as we pray for each other, seek God's help, and practice affirming principles on a daily basis, we can make our marriage a "dream come true."